Presented To:

_____

By:

_____

Date:

_____

GOD'S HAND ON MY SHOULDER FOR WOMEN

Experiencing the Presence of God in Your Everyday Life

HONOR HB BOOKS

Inspiration and Motivation for the Seasons of Life

An Imprint of Cook Communications Ministries • Colorado Springs, CO

08 07 06 05 04   10 9 8 7 6 5 4 3 2 1

God's Hand on My Shoulder for Women
Experiencing the Presence of God in Your Everyday Life
ISBN 1-56292-992-5
Copyright © 2004 Bordon Books
6532 E. 71st Street, Suite 105
Tulsa, OK 74133

Published by Honor Books
An Imprint of Cook Communications Ministries
4050 Lee Vance View
Colorado Springs, CO 80918

Developed by Bordon Books

Manuscript written by The Creative Word.

Introduction

In time of crisis, He is there. In the quiet times, He is there. When you think you're all alone, He is always there.

God's Hand On My Shoulder for Women is a devotional book just for you, filled with encounters with the One who loves you most, along with encouraging reflections to help you experience His presence in your everyday life. God is always with you, but when you suddenly become aware of His presence, everything in your life changes because you are changed from within.

These true-to-life stories and devotional reflections will help you discover how God's transforming presence directs the paths you walk as a woman and wipes away the tears you cry. God is also present to share with you the happiest moments of your life—because He is always there and cares for you deeply. Allow Him to change your life and your heart as you become aware of His hand on your shoulder.

You hide them in the shelter of your presence.
PSALM 31:20 NLT

God's nearness brings safety.

OVERWHELMING ASSURANCE

BARBARA PEEKED INTO THE LIVING ROOM TO FIND JASMINE, HER 18-MONTH-OLD DAUGHTER, EATING CHEERIOS FROM A CUP AND WATCHING A CARTOON. *Oh good,* she thought. *She's busy and I can finally get the dishwasher loaded.*

Only a few minutes had passed as Barbara filled the dishwasher with the breakfast dishes when she heard a voice in her heart say, *Go check on Jasmine.*

Barbara argued. *She's in the living room. She's fine. I just checked on her.* She continued to place glasses in the top rack.

The voice in her heart grew louder. *Hurry, check on Jasmine! Now!*

To no avail, Barbara tried to ignore the prompting in her heart as it grew more insistent. "Okay!" she said aloud.

Slamming the dishwasher shut, she huffed down the hall to the living room. Her toddler no longer sat in front of the television! Panic gripped Barbara's heart and she raced for the stairs. She was horrified at the sight of Jasmine sitting on the top step, blood running from her lips, a razor in her hand!

Jasmine held up the razor like a trophy to her mother. Barbara ran up the stairs and scooped Jasmine into her arms. *God, I'm sorry. I should have listened.*

I am here, God seemed to say. Overwhelming relief flooded Barbara. Even before she washed Jasmine's mouth and found only a tiny cut, she knew God's protection had prompted her to go to her daughter and keep her from further harm.

Have you ever thought you heard God giving you direction but reasoned that it was only your imagination? The next time you feel an inner prompting, respond to it and see what God brings into your life as a result of His hand on your shoulder.

§

Thank You, God, for Your love and protection. Forgive me when I don't listen, and help me to hear Your voice in every situation. You continually offer me the right path to safety. Help me to choose it.

*Jesus answered him, "I tell you the truth,
today you will be with me in paradise."*
LUKE 23:43

Faith is the bridge from this world to the next.

A SIGN IN
THE SKY

IT HAD BEEN A LONG THREE WEEKS SINCE BETH'S MOM,
ESTHER, HAD BEEN ADMITTED INTO THE HOSPICE. Day and
night, Beth kept a vigil by her bedside.

When she could, Esther reminisced with her only daughter about
the memorable moments of their lives. They laughed about the time
when, as a five-year-old, Beth gave the cat a haircut. They reflected on
the many outfits Esther had lovingly hand-sewn for her daughter over
the years. They cried over the loss of Beth's dad only two years earlier.

When it was obvious that Esther's time was close, Beth had one last
request of her mother. She hesitated at first, thinking she might sound
silly. Beth swallowed hard and said, "Mom, I want you to do something
for me . . . when you get to heaven, I mean."

No longer able to speak, Esther took Beth's hand.

Beth continued, "When you get there, and you find Dad, would you
just send me a sign that everything's, well, all right?"

Esther simply squeezed Beth's hand and smiled.

It was evening when Esther peacefully took her last breath. In a daze of exhaustion and grief, Beth walked out the front door of the hospice for the last time. As she paused to breathe in the evening air, something in the sky caught her eye. Looking up, she saw a glittering star. And she knew.

To her the star meant her mother was Home, shining down on her from heaven, saying, "Look, Sweetie, I made it. Dad's here too—and everything is all right."

Have you, like Beth, ever wished for a sign that a loved one has made it safely from this world into Jesus' arms? If Jesus was your loved one's Savior, then you have a sign—it's God's promise found throughout the Bible that anyone who believes in Him will live with Him in heaven forever.

§

God, thank You for Your promise of eternal life for those who believe in You. I look forward to the day when I will be in heaven with You and my loved ones who have gone before me. Until then, help me live every second of my life in a way that is pleasing to You.

In a multitude of counselors there is safety.
PROVERBS 24:6 NKJV

There is more light than can be seen through a window.

LIGHTING
THE WAY

SINCE ALEXANDRIA'S LIGHTHOUSE IN ANCIENT EGYPT, LIGHTHOUSES HAVE LONG STEERED SEAFARERS AWAY FROM DANGER. Their powerful lights warn of rocky coasts, underwater reefs, or sandy shoals that would spell disaster for even the largest, most powerful ship. In ancient times, fires were built atop lighthouses to radiate light toward the sea. Now powerful, sophisticated lighting systems are used to guide ships. Different lighthouses today have their own unique flash patterns so sailors can tell exactly where they are and what specific dangers lurk ahead.

Like navigating the sea, we, too, find ourselves in many potentially disastrous situations as we journey through life. Fortunately, when we're confused, not knowing which way to go, we can call on God, our own personal lighthouse, to show us the way. Wherever we are, He is always there with His hand on our shoulder, directing us throughout our journey.

We can also call on others who have "been there, done that" for help.

They, too, are like lighthouses, able to provide valuable direction for life. It is well worth your time as a Christian woman to cultivate friends you can trust to give you good counsel about life's dilemmas. For example, a woman who has done a good job raising her own children would be an ideal source of help as you navigate the rough waters of parenting. Or a woman whose business savvy you admire could direct you safely through the treacherous reef of office politics.

Lighthouses for life are all around you. And they're more than willing to help you make it safely to your destination. All you need to do is look for their shining lights and steer your ship in their direction.

Christians who have lived and experienced life offer much in the way of friendship and counsel. And usually they are more than happy to isten, to share, and to advise. Seek their light for the journey.

§

Lord, You remind us in so many ways that we are to hold up one another and to allow others to hold us up when we need it. Thank You for the beautiful fellowship of believers and their wise counsel and special friendship.

"I know the plans I have for you," declares the LORD,
"plans to prosper you and not to harm you,
plans to give you hope and a future."
JEREMIAH 29:11

A possibility is a hint from God.

JUDY'S "SURPRISE" JOB

JUDY PLACED TWO QUARTERS ON THE CONVENIENCE STORE COUNTER AND LEFT WITH A COPY OF THE SUNDAY PAPER. It was a routine she had followed after church every week for the past five months.

As a single mom of two, Judy had a tough time making ends meet. It was hard enough keeping the kids in shoes. Now the car needed a new water pump, and the microwave was on the fritz.

Although Judy liked her teacher's aid job at the elementary school, it just wasn't paying enough. As she scanned the classifieds, her thoughts were familiar: Not qualified for that one . . . Over-qualified for that one . . . That's even less money than I'm making now . . . .

Judy's eyes suddenly locked on an ad she had seen in the previous Sunday classifieds but had skipped over. It was for a cook at a retirement center. She had never done anything remotely similar. Yet she couldn't get the ad out of her mind. It was as if God was telling her, *This is it.*

This is the job I have for you. She ignored the prompting for a couple of days, but it grew stronger. She finally picked up the phone and called the center.

Weeks later, as she prepared for her job as cook at the Mira Flora Retirement Center, Judy knelt to thank God for this "surprise" job. It was, in fact, the best job she'd ever had, and the salary was more than enough to meet her family's needs. *Who knew?* she thought. *I did,* God answered in her heart.

Is God leading you to take a direction in life that seems illogical or impossible? Have confidence in His leading. Remember, He made you, He loves you, and He knows what's best for you, even if it doesn't make sense at the time.

§

*God, I trust you. I know You love me and have the best plan
for my life. Help me slow down, quiet my mind, and pay attention
to Your voice as You prompt my heart and guide me into
Your perfect will.*

God places the lonely in families.
PSALM 68:6 NLT

The heart is happiest that beats for others.

A FAMILY FOR MARINA

AFTER YEARS OF LOOKING, 40-YEAR-OLD MARINA STILL HADN'T FOUND HER "KNIGHT IN SHINING ARMOR." She was willing to accept that she might never get married (much to her mother's disappointment), but there was an unshakable desire in her heart to have children.

Her friends suggested that Marina try the international adoption route, but she wasn't sure. *I know there are lots of kids in the world who need a home, but can I love a child who's not really my own?* When she learned about a mission trip to a Russian orphanage, Marina jumped at the opportunity to go. She hoped the experience would help her decide about adoption.

Marina was shocked by the poverty of the orphanage's surrounding community. The orphanage itself, though clean and orderly, was dismally poor. Marina was particularly drawn to a thin, quiet girl with big brown eyes. It took her most of the first day just to get the girl to come close to her. When she finally, hesitantly, slid into a chair next to her, Marina called the interpreter over and began to ask the girl questions.

"What is your name?"

"Marina," she said softly.

"That's my name, too!" Marina beamed.

"How old are you?" The girl held up seven fingers.

Marina laughed as she slowly hugged the girl close. At that moment she knew, without a doubt, that she and this beautiful, dark-eyed girl who shared her name, were meant to be family.

With God there are no coincidental surprises. He orchestrates even the most minute details. Are you willing to discover what He has in store for your life today?

§

Oh Lord, I want to seek You and Your ways for my life. Help me to let go of my need to control, and to allow You to bring the people and circumstances into my life that show just how much You love me. Thank You for special surprises

*To him who is able to do immeasurably more
than all we ask or imagine . . . to him be glory . . .
for ever and ever!*
EPHESIANS 3:20-21

**The greater your confidence in God,
the more abundantly you receive whatever you ask.**

ASK WITH CONFIDENCE

"DADDY, FIX IT,"—THE CONFIDENT REQUEST OF A CHILD. Perhaps you remember making the same request as you parked a broken tricycle in front of your dad or dropped a doll missing its right leg into his lap. You didn't think twice. Whenever something went wrong, you simply expected Dad to perform a miracle.

As we grow older, our faith in Dad to fix the things that go wrong in life dims. Dad is only human, and the realization that his miracle-working ability is pretty much limited to fixing broken toys and scaring away the bears under your bed is a hard lesson to learn. As much as he'd like to, Dad can't fix it when your company goes bankrupt and you're suddenly jobless, when you find out that the lump is malignant, or when your husband of 25 years decides the grass is greener elsewhere.

However, that doesn't mean that having someone to turn to when things go wrong is just a passing benefit of childhood. God's ever-present help is available every day. He's just waiting to be asked. Long after you stopped relying on your earthly father to work miracles, your heavenly Father was there to take over—to do more for you than you could ever ask or imagine possible. God wants you to come to Him like you would your dad—to boldly walk up to His throne, drop whatever is wrong in your life into His lap and say with childlike confidence, "Daddy, please fix it."

Are there parts of your life that you think are too broken for God to fix? Don't lose heart. Our heavenly Father is able, and He wants to make you whole again.

$

God, I admit that it is difficult for me to come to You at times with my problems. Forgive me when I forget that You are bigger than any problem or concern I have, and that You stand ready to help. Help me to trust You with all of my life.

The godly are concerned for the welfare of their animals.
PROVERBS 12:10 NLT

All creatures great and small, the good Lord loves them all.

ALFALFA'S BIG ADVENTURE

"HERE, ALFALFA! HERE, KITTY, KITTY!" JENNIFER CALLED AS SHE WALKED THROUGH THE NEIGHBORHOOD. She had been looking for her missing cat all afternoon, even offering to pay a couple of the neighbor kids to help her in the search.

When it grew dark, Jennifer went home, sat in her rocking chair, and cried. She blamed herself for leaving the door open while she went outside to wish her neighbors a safe trip. They were packing a U-Haul truck for a move to Alaska.

As she rocked and cried she prayed for God's protection over the cat that she had rescued as a tiny kitten from the animal shelter and had named after her favorite Little Rascals character. She knew it would be hard to sleep without the furry, purring bundle curled up at the foot of the bed.

After five anxious days and still no sign of Alfalfa, Jennifer could not resign herself to the fact that she would never see her cat again. Repeatedly she felt God near. It was as if He were saying, "Don't give up."

Then on the sixth day, she received a phone call. It was from her neighbors who had moved to Alaska—with a stowaway in their U-Haul. Jennifer couldn't believe it. Alfalfa had sneaked aboard the truck and made the three-thousand-mile trip. Her neighbors reported that the cat was hungry and thirsty, but other than that, seemed to be fine.

When Jennifer picked up Alfalfa at the baggage claim counter at the airport, she hugged him with relief and thanked God for bringing him safely home from his big adventure.

Have you ever felt silly or hurt when something you love doesn't seem important to anyone else? Rest assured that what's important to you is always important to God. He cares for all His creatures, and He cares for you.

§

Thank You, Lord, for giving to me a heart that beats with compassion for all of Your living creatures. Thank You for enriching my life with the wonder and company of pets. Help me to be a good steward of that which You have entrusted to my care.

*Always give thanks for everything to God the Father
in the name of our Lord Jesus Christ.*
EPHESIANS 5:20 NLT

Friendships are discovered rather than made.

FROM CAR TROUBLE TO FRIENDSHIP

IT'S A PIECE OF JUNK, SUSAN THOUGHT WHEN THE MECHANIC GAVE HER THE BAD NEWS ABOUT HER CAR. It had been nothing but trouble from the day she drove it off the lot, and now it would be in the shop for a full week.

Independent to the extreme, Susan hated more than anything to ask other people for help but she didn't have a choice. Susan called Nancy, an acquaintance from work who lived in her neighborhood. She apologetically asked Nancy if she could ride with her to and from the office for the next week.

During their 30-minute commutes, Susan and Nancy talked about everything from problems with their bosses to which stores had the best shoe sales. When they learned they were both Christians, the two also talked about their faith and shared favorite Scriptures. The time they spent in the car flew by, and the occasional traffic jam went unnoticed.

On Friday after work, Nancy took Susan to the mechanic's garage to pick up her repaired car. Before leaving, Susan told Nancy how much she had enjoyed their time together that week. Nancy said that she too would miss their "car"versations and joked that if they were fortunate, Susan's car would break down again soon.

The next Monday, as Susan drove to work, she was surprised to find herself actually thanking God for her car that only a week earlier she had wanted to drive off the nearest cliff. In the midst of inconvenience, God had directed her to a new friendship. *Thank you, God. I never would have gotten to know Nancy otherwise*, she thought.

Sometimes we fail to see the forest for the trees. Have you ever dreaded something that later resulted in a great experience? Learn to see God's power and blessings in those unexpected situations.

$

Oh God, You are sovereign and true. Forgive me for my shortsightedness and doubt. Thank You for blessing me with the wonderful friends that You bring across my path. Help me to see life from Your perspective.

*I will praise thee; for I am fearfully
and wonderfully made: marvelous are thy works;
and that my soul knoweth right well.*
PSALM 139:14 KJV

God made us and we wonder at it.

WHAT AM I WORTH?

A POPULAR TELEVISION PROGRAM, THE ANTIQUES ROAD SHOW, FEATURES ANTIQUE SPECIALISTS WHO TRAVEL TO DIFFERENT TOWNS ACROSS THE COUNTRY. People in these towns are invited to bring items for evaluation that they suspect might be valuable antiques.

Suspense builds as a specialist inspects a specific piece—what era it's from, where it came from, and what it was used for. Finally, they reveal what the owner is anxious to hear—how much it's worth. It's often surprising that a piece—say a beautiful, ornate lamp that appears to be priceless—is worth only a little. Yet another piece—like a crudely carved wooden doll that appears to be worth nothing—is valued at hundreds of dollars.

Likewise, there are so many situations in life they make you feel that your value is uncertain and dependent on someone else's opinion. Will your boss think you're worth a raise? Will the people in your new neighborhood think you're worth getting to know? Will your children think you're worth coming to for advice?

Fortunately, you don't have to live in suspense, wondering what your value is to God. He values you so much that He sacrificed His only Son's life to have an eternal relationship with you. No matter what happens in life, no matter when or where you feel your value is uncertain, God's hand is always on your shoulder, and He's whispering in your ear, *You're priceless to Me, and ultimately, only My opinion matters.*

Think about the miracle of new life born into the world every day, multiple times each minute. God, the Creator of all, values every life. There is no one like you—nor has there ever been, nor will there ever be again. You are incredibly special!

Lord, there are times when I feel small and unworthy. When that happens, help me to turn my eyes toward You, the One who fashioned me into the unique person I am. When I think of Your Son who gave His life in exchange for mine, I realize just how much I mean to You. Thank You.

*In every thing by prayer and supplication
with thanksgiving let your requests
be made known unto God.*
PHILIPPIANS 4:6 KJV

It is impossible on reasonable grounds to disbelieve miracles.

SECONDS, ANYONE?

THE MEMBERS OF THE CHURCH BOARD AGREED—PAM AND DEBBIE HAD A GREAT IDEA. Convicted by the Bible's commands to care for the poor and needy, the two women had brainstormed ways to serve those less fortunate in their community. A soup kitchen seemed the perfect solution to share Christ's love in a tangible way.

Pam and Debbie worked hard recruiting volunteers to help in the kitchen, and they posted flyers, inviting people to come. They made the most of their limited budget and felt good about the amount of food they had prepared for the kitchen's first day.

They felt good, that is, until they saw how many people lined up outside, waiting for the doors to open. The two women swallowed hard then looked at each other, thinking, Uh-oh, we don't have enough food for them all. "We better pray," Pam said. The two women held hands as they prayed that people's appetites would shrink before they came through the door!

Soon Pam, Debbie, and the other volunteers busily greeted and served their guests. When everyone had been served, the workers were amazed to see their food supply undiminished. Hadn't they just given heaping plates of food to more than 100 people? And yet, the serving dishes were still full. There was more than enough for their guests to have seconds.

Afterward, Pam and Debbie hugged each other and cried. They were left speechless by the awesome miracle God performed that day in their humble soup kitchen. It was as if God Himself had served the food, replenishing every spoonful as each one was spooned out. Pam and Debbie were sure He had been there all along.

It's reassuring to know that just as He did in biblical times, God continues to multiply your simple efforts, bringing ample supply to all who seek Him. Never forget to bring your requests to Him, and know that He will hear and answer.

§

Father, just as You revealed Your power and mercy through Your Son, Jesus Christ, when He fed five thousand with only five loaves of bread and two fish, help me to believe in Your power to do the same today. Help me to trust and obey Your Holy Spirit always and remember that You are always near.

Rejoice in the Lord, you who are righteous,
and praise his holy name.
PSALM 97:12

As the purse is emptied, the heart is filled.

A MIRACLE ON 52ND STREET

FINANCES WERE ESPECIALLY TIGHT THIS MONTH IN THE SMITH HOME. With two teenagers, it seemed like any money Angela and her husband brought home went right back out the door for school fees, braces, music lessons, and the myriad of other needs that teens have. Angela was diligent about looking for ways to make the grocery allowance go as far as possible.

On this particular grocery day, Angela had carefully written out her list. She knew she had just enough cash to cover everything on the list. However, when she pulled up at a traffic light on her way to the store, she saw a man on the corner begging from those in the stopped cars. She often saw homeless people begging on this corner of 52nd Street, and Angela usually just waved them on. But this man caught her attention.

On the cardboard sign he carried was written "Rejoice in the Lord always!" Something about that sign touched Angela's heart. Before she knew it, she had rolled down her window and handed the man a $5 bill. Driving on, she sighed, Oh well, I guess I can adjust the grocery list, or put it all on a credit card . . . .

Later, standing in the grocery store check-out line, Angela pulled out her wallet and was astonished to find that in place of the $5 bill she had given to the man on the corner was a crisp new $20 bill. As she pulled it out of her wallet, she felt the breath of God when He said to her heart, *Don't be surprised. I delight in rewarding My children for their faithfulness.* All the way home, she rejoiced in the Lord.

Have you, like Angela, ever been tempted to remain focused on your own agenda instead of recognizing God's purposes? Maybe it's worth slowing down long enough to see the divine appointments He often presents. You, too, may be amazed at the outcome!

§

God, forgive me when I tend to be selfish instead of generous. Help me to see You in every person I meet. Prepare my heart to share with others from whatever little I may have, and to know that You will supply my every need. And may my motivation to do so always be genuine and selfless.

Whatever you ask in My name, that I will do.
JOHN 14:13 NKJV

We give God the name of good; but it is
only by shortening "good" that it becomes "God."

THE AWESOME NAME OF GOD

IN MEDIEVAL TIMES, BEFORE JOHANNES GUTENBERG INVENTED THE PRINTING PRESS, SCRIPTURE WAS DUPLICATED BY HAND. Monks in Europe's monasteries spent their lives painstakingly copying the Bible, word for word, with a quill pen and ink. They also often decorated the pages with beautiful, colorful creations; some in gold. Today, we find examples of these beautiful manuscripts in museums throughout the world.

The medieval monks took their work of transcribing God's Word very seriously, approaching their task with great reverence and awe. In fact, whenever they came to the word God, they would stop, bathe, and put on clean clothes. Then they would pray and write the word with a brand new quill.

The monks of old understood the power of the name of God. In His name the Red Sea was parted, fives loaves of bread and two fish were used to feed 5,000 people, and the blind were given back their sight. Most important, in His name Jesus was raised from the dead, securing forever our promise of eternal life.

That same awesome power is available to us today. In fact, it is ours to claim every second of every day. And we don't have to bathe or put on clean clothes. All we have to do to enjoy God's presence is call on His name. We may not need to part a sea or feed 5,000 people, but the Bible promises that anything we ask in God's name He will do—heal the hurt of a broken marriage, restore a rebellious child, provide for our material needs. The name of God is the world's greatest power source!

Though we can never fully comprehend God, we can begin to understand His nature because He reveals Himself to us through Scripture. God is omnipresent, unchanging in character, and ever victorious. His purposes are always accomplished. What assurance!

§

Dear Father, Your name is more precious than gold; more reassuring than the dawn. Your powerful presence sustains me through every trial and heartache. And Your grace and mercy provide me peace, joy, and hope. I love You, O God, and I want to honor and serve You all the days of my life.

In the eighth year of his reign,
while he was still young, he began
to seek the God of his father David.
2 CHRONICLES 34:3

There is nothing small in the service of God.

OPERATION AMBER

THANK GOODNESS DIANE JOHNSON HAD GONE THROUGH HER ENTIRE PREGNANCY AND DELIVERY BEFORE DAVID WAS LAID OFF, WHEN THEY LOST MEDICAL INSURANCE. Now baby Amber was six months old, and David was still out of work. The Johnsons were barely scraping by on unemployment benefits.

As difficult as life was for the Johnsons, it took a turn for the worse when Amber was diagnosed with leukemia. Although David was a perfect donor match for a bone marrow transplant, there seemed to be no way the Johnsons could afford the expensive procedure. Facing an uncertain future, Diane and David asked everyone in their church—even the junior high Sunday School class they taught—to pray for a miracle for Amber.

Little did the Johnsons know that their jr. high class of only eight members decided to do more than pray for Amber. They began projects to raise money for a transplant operation. They held bake sales, car washes, and special collections at their school. Their determination soon caught the attention of the local media, and they were invited to talk about their cause on TV and radio programs. Before long, the whole town knew about baby Amber, and contributions poured into a special bank account set up specifically for her operation.

After the bone marrow transplant was pronounced a complete success, and Amber's life had received a brand-new prognosis, Diane and David marveled at God's great power and love. They knew God was very near throughout it all. Their class had shone light into a dark place. God's hand rested on the determination found in the hearts of a few kids and on the life of this family.

God's people come in all shapes, sizes, colors, and ages. And He values and uses every person in whatever stage he or she is in life. Look for the beautiful miracles God will do through those whom you may least expect.

God, may I never forget You came to earth in the form of an infant so that I may have life eternal. May this knowledge remind me of the value You place in both the young and the small, knowing Your power will always be manifested through a willing heart.

How do you know what will happen tomorrow?
For your life is like the morning fog—it's here
for a little while, then it's gone. What you ought
to say is, "If the Lord wants us to,
we will live and do this or that."
JAMES 4:14-15 NLT

There are no disappointments to those
whose wills are buried in the will of God.

ANDREA'S
DISAPPOINTING
WEEKEND

ANDREA COULDN'T BE MORE DISAPPOINTED. The store
manager had just announced that the quarterly inventory schedule had
been moved up a week. As usual during inventory week, Andrea and all
the other employees would have to work both Saturday and Sunday. Of
course, she was always glad for overtime pay, but the new schedule con-
flicted with the women's retreat that she'd been looking forward to for so
long.

It was going to be a great time—a whole weekend away at a first-class
lodge in the mountains. The speakers were also first-class, and a couple
of popular Christian artists were scheduled to provide entertainment

and inspiration. It was no wonder that the reservations list was filled soon after the retreat was announced. There was even a waiting list in case someone—like Andrea—cancelled.

The whole weekend of the retreat, Andrea moped. Taking inventory had never been more tedious. Even worse, the next Sunday at church, the retreat attendees couldn't wait to share their stories. Andrea was definitely feeling sorry for herself. That is, until one woman shared the exciting news that she had accepted Jesus as Savior at the retreat. She also revealed that she was originally on the waiting list and it was only because someone else had cancelled that she was able to go in the first place.

Andrea's perspective immediately took a new turn. She felt God's smile warm her heart as she thanked Him for using her disappointment for someone else's eternal good!

There is no denying that disappointments hurt. But our attitude toward the things we cannot change can also help us accept them and move on without bitterness. And sometimes, we'll discover a reason to be glad.

§

God, You know the pain of disappointment. We have disappointed You time and time again. Yet You love us so much You don't dwell on the disappointment of the moment. Teach me to do likewise. Help me to develop an eternal perspective for every circumstance.

In this you greatly rejoice, even though now for a little while . . . you have been distressed by various trials, so that the proof of your faith, being more precious than gold . . . even though tested by fire, may be found to result in praise and glory and honor at the revelation of Jesus Christ.

1 PETER 1:6-7 NASB

She who suffers much will know much.

PURE AS GOLD

SINCE LONG BEFORE CHRIST WAS BORN, PEOPLE HAVE PURSUED ONE OF THE WORLD'S GREATEST TREASURES—GOLD. But extracting this valuable metal from the earth is a complicated process. Gold is typically embedded in rock, and through the centuries, various methods have been used to separate gold from rock into its pure form.

Like gold, we too must go through a life-long process to refine our character. God doesn't bring life's hardships, but uses them to point out our impurities—our sinful tendencies. Then with His hand always on our shoulder, He guides us in the process of separating ourselves from sin to become more like Him. The more impurities you eliminate from your life, the more purely Christ-like you become.

As a Christian you desire to attain many of the qualities that make gold so valuable. For example, gold is one of the shiniest metals. In fact, its chemical symbol, Au, comes from aurum, the Latin word for shining dawn. The more your Christian character is refined, the more you shine for Christ.

Gold is also the most malleable of all metals, meaning it can be molded into various shapes without breaking; it is an excellent conductor of electricity, and it does not dissolve or rust. Likewise, the more pure our character, the more God is able to mold us to His will, the better we are able to convey His love to others, and the less we are prone to be tarnished by outside influences. The refining process is a difficult one, but God is there, right by your side to see you through anything you face. And the end result is definitely worthwhile!

No one likes to endure the process of burning away the impurities of our human nature. Yet it must happen so we can become more Christ-like in our character. We, like gold, must undergo the great pressure that produces a heart pure and useful for God's Kingdom.

§

Lord, I want to be useful. I want to be poured out. I want to serve others, thus demonstrating my love and devotion to You. And yet I know my pride, self-righteousness, stubbornness, and prejudices prevent me from reflecting Your image. These and more must be chipped away from my heart. Be with me always, and give me strength to withstand the crucible of Your love, making me useful for Your Kingdom.

Be ready with a meal or a bed when it's needed. Why, some have
extended hospitality to angels without ever knowing it!
HEBREWS 13:2 MSG

She who gives a little with a smile
gives more than she who gives much with a frown.

THE TRAIN
STATION ANGEL

AN ART HISTORY MAJOR, KRISTEN CELEBRATED HER
GRADUATION WITH A TOUR OF EUROPE'S GREAT MUSEUMS.
After a glorious week touring the Louvre in Paris, she boarded a train,
Italy-bound. She couldn't wait to see the art treasures of Florence and
Rome.

Kristen's itinerary required a train change, but somehow she miscal-
culated and stepped off at the wrong stop. She found herself in a station,
in a city she'd never heard of before. To top it off, it was nighttime, and
she'd left her *French Dictionary for Travelers* on the train.

An older woman, sweeping the floor of the now-deserted station,
noticed the girl's look of despair and spoke to her. Using the most creative hand signs she could think of, Kristen tried to communicate that
she was going to Italy. The woman just shook her head, turned, and left.
Kristen sighed. Obviously, she would have to spend the night in the station and hope that tomorrow someone would be able to direct her to the

right train.

After a few minutes, the woman returned with a basket of bread and cheese for Kristen. She also had a train schedule that Kristen used to determine the train she needed to board and its departure time the next morning. Suddenly, she no longer felt alone. As she quietly munched on the bread and cheese she felt very close to God—as though He sat right next to her. God's protective hand had brought provision and direction through this woman's kindness. And He himself seemed to be sharing a very quiet moment with her.

Over the years, Kristen forgot many of the details of her trip to Europe, but she never forgot the woman in the train station, the unlikely angel who had helped her get back on the right track.

Feeling vulnerable can provide opportunity for spiritual growth, but oftentimes we resist others' help. Only when we empty ourselves of self-sufficiency can we see the necessity of dependency on Almighty God. That's exactly where He wants us to be.

֍

Father, forgive my arrogance when I think I don't need anyone's help—including Yours. Show me how Your provisions come through the support and compassion of others, especially when I am out of my comfort zone of familiarity. Thank You for using others to help me.

When she finds it you can be sure
she'll call her friends and neighbors:
"Celebrate with me! I found my lost coin!"
Count on it—that's the kind of party God's angels
throw every time one lost soul turns to God.
LUKE 15:9-10 MSG

Real beauty is never lost.

THE LOST
RING

NO MORE PROCRASTINATION. Valerie marked Saturday the 20th on the calendar and proclaimed it Closet Clean-Up Day. Over the years, her three children had collected enough stuff to fill a football stadium, and she was determined to get rid of it—or at least make a dent in it.

On the appointed Saturday, Valerie gave each child plastic trash bags, some designated for Good Will and some for trash. Valerie floated from room to room, encouraging and lending a hand to the reluctant workers. At the end of the day, the bags—13 in all—were dragged out to the garage.

While Valerie lavished praise on her children for a job well done, she came to a devastating realization—her heirloom ring, the one that had been in her family for three generations, was gone. Frantic, she began tearing through the house, pulling cushions off chairs, looking in potted plants, and scouring through drawers. The ring could be anywhere.

Valerie was on the verge of despair when her seven-year-old, Benjamin, suggested that they pray about it. Valerie, and then each child in turn, made a brief plea to God for the safe return of the ring. A calm assurance flooded Valerie's heart. *God knows where my ring is, and He will lead us to it,* she thought. No sooner had they finished praying than Benjamin said, "Mom, I know where it is." He went straight to the garage, Valerie close behind, and pulled one of the bags from the pile. "It's in here. I just know it."

Skeptical, Valerie opened the bag and emptied out the contents—including her ring. Relieved and thankful, she felt as though God had directed Benjamin with His hand to the exact location of the ring. Perhaps He had.

Just when everything seems lost, God provides a reason to rejoice—think of it as a glimpse of heaven's glory!

§

Heavenly Father, I admit I lose hope at times and fall into despair instead of turning to You for solace and direction. And although at times the best thing for me to do is to accept my circumstances with grace, I thank You for revealing to me Your glory through small miracles.

*What is faith? It is the confident assurance
that what we hope for is going to happen.
It is the evidence of things we cannot yet see.*
HEBREWS 11:1 NLT

What is faith unless it is to believe what you do not see.

THE CONFIDENCE
TO LEAP

AFRICA IS HOME TO SOME OF THE WORLD'S MOST FAS-
CINATING ANIMALS. The lean, sleek cheetah is the world's fastest
animal, able to reach speeds up to 60 miles per hour. The lumbering ele-
phant, which can weigh more than six tons, is the world's largest land
animal. The secretive leopard's night vision is six times better than a
human's.

The African impala is equally fascinating. It can jump to a height of
over 10 feet and, in the same jump, cover a distance of more than 30
feet. However, this amazing animal can be safely kept in a zoo, enclosed
by a wall only three feet high. Why? Because an impala will not jump if
it cannot see where its feet will land.

Life often requires us to take risks—to jump without knowing where
our feet will land. We risk losing friends when we refuse to join them in
an activity that's not pleasing to God. We risk disappointment when we
make career moves. We risk rejection from our children when we disci-

pline them. Yet God often prompts our hearts to make such risky jumps.

Fortunately, faith gives us the confidence we need to conquer our fear and jump. God promised that if you take a risk in faith, He will make sure that you experience a safe landing. God doesn't want us to be limited by the small, three-feet-tall barriers in life. He desires for you to experience His presence and take hold of His hand and jump, trusting Him with all your heart and soul for the outcome.

Life requires risks from time to time. Such opportunities are faith-building exercises. Even if things don't go as planned, risks strengthen and confirm our faith. Risks are worthwhile if we include God in the process.

§

Father, help me to discern the risks that are worth taking. Help me to remember to always include You in the process and to listen for Your voice. In so doing, I can rest assured that no matter the outcome, You are with me.

A word aptly spoken is like apples of gold in settings of silver.
PROVERBS 25:11

Correction does much, but encouragement does more.

SHANNA'S BIG WIN

SHANNA HAD BITTEN OFF ALL HER NAILS. Her son's baseball game was not going well. It was only the second inning and already Bryce had walked several batters and missed two grounders that should have been easy outs. He wasn't the only one experiencing a bad game. The outfield players were dropping balls, and the short stop was letting way too many slip past.

From the stands Brenda, the short stop's mother, hollered at her son Nathan, "I can't believe you missed that one! Are you asleep? You're looking like a loser out there!"

Shanna thought Bryce could use a little "encouragement" too. A couple of times she opened her mouth to yell something, but a voice inside told her not to do it. She found it difficult to watch her son and his team fail so miserably, but she resisted the urge to follow Brenda's example.

When the game was finally—thankfully—over, Shanna and Bryce followed Brenda and Nathan to the parking lot. Brenda continued her tirade about her son's embarrassing performance, threatening to ground him if the next game wasn't better. Shanna and Bryce walked, wordlessly, to their car. As they drove home, Bryce said, "Mom, I know we didn't do very good today, but thank you for not hollering at me."

Then Shanna felt the same inner voice that had told her to keep quiet during the game. God's gentle nudge now prompted her to speak up, "Honey, I think you're a winner no matter how your baseball games go."

It's easy to know the answers when you're sitting on the sidelines. But it's the efforts of those willing to risk failure that win the prize. Instead of pointing out their faults in the process, strive to be the one who lifts them up during their challenges, offering encouragement instead of criticism, no matter the outcome.

§

God, You are the ultimate fan. Like a loving parent, You cheer me on,
instilling in me the courage to keep trying and reassuring me of Your
love no matter what. And when life isn't going as I hoped,
You are more than a moral supporter. You gently wipe my tears, mend
my broken heart, and instill in me the strength to go on.
Help me to learn Your ways; being ever faithful to model
unconditional love to those around me.

You're blessed when you're at the end of your rope.
With less of you there is more of God and his rule . . .
You're blessed when you're content with just who you are—
no more, no less. That's the moment you find yourselves
proud owners of everything that can't be bought.
MATTHEW 5:3-5 MSG

One heart is mirror to another.

GRACE IN ACTION

JO LOVED THE DOWNTOWN CHURCH SHE ATTENDED. A hundred-year-old building with beautiful stained glass windows and ornately carved pews. The acoustics in the sanctuary were a singer's dream, and Jo imagined that the choir sounded just like heaven's choir of angels. Unlike Jo, who was solidly middle-class, other church members were primarily wealthy. Among the women, Sundays were fashion shows—especially Easter Sunday.

That's why the stranger stood out.

One Easter, she shuffled in during the first hymn and slipped into a pew at the front of the church. She was dressed in tatters, her hair was unkempt, and it was obvious she hadn't bathed recently. The members were shaken by her presence. Their whispering and fidgeting refused to go unnoticed by most.

During the part of the service when the congregation was invited to greet those around them, Jo hesitated, but then followed the prompting in her heart. She left her seat and moved down front to greet the woman. She patted her on the arm and warmly welcomed her to Main Street Church. Then she sat by the woman for the rest of the service, sharing her Bible and hymnal with her. Others in the congregation were shocked, but the pastor was impressed. Afterward, he caught up with Jo to thank her for showing hospitality to their poor guest.

Jo explained, "You don't understand. I was once homeless too. But a kind Christian couple took me in and helped me find a new start. God gave me a little opportunity today to return the favor."

Christ gave His life for all—even those we may fail to notice or those we believe undeserving. The only way they or anyone will ever realize how much He loves them is if we are willing to love them just where they are. Look for ways to represent Christ's compassion to everyone, every day.

§

God, It's easy to forget that I, too, was broken, alone, and afraid until Jesus extended His hand of love and forgiveness to me. And that has made all the difference. Fill me with the courage and compassion to reach out to others who are where I was. Help me to show them who You are in me, and may they desire to know You as their Savior as a result of meeting me.

The very hairs of your head are all numbered.
MATTHEW 10:30 NASB

God loves each of us as if there were only one of us.

HEAVENLY NUMBERS

HAVE YOU EVER THOUGHT ABOUT HOW MUCH NUMBERS AFFECT OUR LIVES? We check the Top 10 List to see which books we should read. Box-office numbers influence our movie-viewing decisions. The lower the number, the better we feel when we're trying on jeans. And nothing's a bigger magnet than a 50 percent off sign in the window of our favorite shoe store.

There are some important numbers in the Bible that God designed to play a vital role in our lives. The 10 Commandments are the first. Given to us thousands of years ago, this list of God's Top 10 Rules is as relevant today as it was then.

And what about the nine beatitudes in Matthew 5:3-12? Jesus promises that the traits mentioned in this passage—such as meekness, mercy, and purity of heart—are rewarded by God with very specific blessings. Another important "nine," the nine fruits of the Spirit found in Galatians 5:22—love, joy, peace, patience, kindness, goodness, faithfulness, gentleness, and self-control. The apostle Paul reminds us that if God's Spirit is in control of our lives, these characteristics will be the evidence.

Finally, don't forget that the Bible says God loves His children so much, He knows a number that no one else in the world can possibly know—the exact number of hairs on each of our heads. Imagine that!

Certainly a God who keeps track of the number of hairs on your head is interested in every detail of your life. Take time to recognize Him in even the simplest task in your day. He is ready to share with you. Invite Him to be a part of all you do.

It's awe-inspiring to think God knows each of us so intimately that He considers each hair on our heads as precious and significant. There are six billion people in our world, yet God loves you as if you were His only child, and He knows every detail about you!

❦

God, it reassures me to realize that I am more than a number to You. You know me, my faults, my prejudices . . . and yet, You love me with an undying love that is beyond comprehension. Help me to see You with my whole heart so I can learn to trust You more.

She carefully watches all that goes on in her household . . .
Her children stand and bless her. Her husband praises her:
'There are many virtuous and capable women in the world,
but you surpass them all!'"
PROVERBS 31:27-29 NLT

The loveliest masterpiece of the heart of God is the heart of a mother.

COMMITMENT OVERLOAD

LINDA'S CHURCH RECENTLY VOTED HER VOLUNTEER OF THE YEAR. It was an easy win. No one else came close to the hours Linda put in to manage the food pantry, teach a Bible study, sing in the choir, and chair the membership committee. It seemed that Linda was at church every night of the week. Most evenings she threw dinner (usually take out) onto the table, wolfed down her food, then dashed out the door to the next commitment.

One Wednesday evening, Linda's friend Beth caught up with her after choir practice. "You must be really proud of Jason," she said. At her friend's confused expression, Beth explained that Linda's son had been recognized at a school assembly the day before for his academic achievement. Beth had attended the assembly to see her daughter receive an award and assumed Linda was in the audience as well.

When Linda got home, she called Jason into the den. When she asked why he hadn't told her about the awards assembly, he shrugged. "Mom, you're always so busy. I didn't think you had time for that kind of stuff."

Jason's words resounded in Linda's heart with a message straight from God. *Your church commitments—worthy as they are—are costing you your family. I want you to be a good wife and mother first, then use whatever time is left over for what I ask you to do.*

Linda hugged her son, apologized for her neglect, and promised to do better in the future. Then she called the pastor to resign as food pantry coordinator and took a few minutes to thank God for His direction and correction. She asked her boys if she could join them in a game of pool.

Sometimes it's difficult to see what is really important, in our busy lives. Activity may produce recognition and feelings of significance, but putting first things first requires us to consider all areas of life—especially our important relationships. They give us something nothing else can replicate: love.

§

Forgive me, Lord, when I become consumed with my own importance. Teach me to find balance in my activities, but never at the expense of my family. Help me to put first things first, beginning with You.

Gray hair is a crown of splendor; it is attained by a righteous life.
PROVERBS 16:31

None are so old as those who have outlived enthusiasm.

MYRTLE'S MESSAGE

ALLISON HATED TO SIT NEXT TO TALKATIVE PEOPLE ON THE AIRPLANE. She traveled frequently for her job as a sales representative. And after making presentations all day, the last thing she wanted was to talk to another person. She usually buried her nose in a magazine, hoping that whomever sat beside her would get the hint. Sometimes, like today, they didn't.

A gray-haired woman with twinkling eyes sat down next to Allison, introduced herself as Myrtle, and announced that she was on her way to see her grandchildren in Phoenix. Then she asked if Allison would like to see photos of her grandchildren. Without waiting for an answer, Myrtle pulled a little book of photos out of her bag. Allison couldn't have been more annoyed.

But before long, Allison found herself telling the old woman all about her job, husband, church, and even about her desire to have children. There was just something about Myrtle and her twinkling eyes that made Allison open up.

When the flight was over—all too soon—Allison thanked Myrtle for listening to her. Myrtle insisted that it was her pleasure, and before they parted, she said with a wink, "Honey, it's a little-known secret. Old people have a lot to give."

Allison thought about what Myrtle said and knew it was a message from heaven. She determined to get to know some of the senior women in her church, and she thanked God for using Myrtle to open her eyes to the friendship that older women have to offer.

You never know when or where you might find a hidden treasure. See everyone—young or old, wealthy or poor—with something worthwhile to give or to receive. You'll become richer in the process!

§

Friendship is one of the greatest blessings you have given to us, Lord. Instill in me qualities of faithfulness so I may be the kind of friend others need. May I also learn to see beyond age or status, making new friends wherever I may go.

We all, with unveiled face,
beholding as in a mirror the glory of the Lord,
are being transformed into the same image
from glory to glory, just as by the Spirit of the Lord.
2 CORINTHIANS 3:18 NKJV

Be what thou seemest! Live thy creed!

SEE YOURSELF IN GOD'S MIRROR

EVERY CARNIVAL HAS ONE—A FUN HOUSE. It's a maze of mirrors that distort your appearance in a variety of ways. One mirror makes you look tall and thin, another short and fat. In one mirror your body appears to be fractured into segments, and in another it looks fluid and wavy. You won't find a mirror in a Fun House that reflects your true appearance.

There are times in the Fun House of life when we're uncertain about who we really are and which way we should go. When we reach these times of confusion, we are often tempted to reflect the image the world holds up to us. For example, we may be tempted to reflect the world's image of a successful business woman—no matter who we have to step on to climb the corporate ladder. Sometimes we're tempted to reflect the image of wealth—no matter how much we go into debt. Perhaps we're tempted to reflect the image of the perfect mother—no matter what we have to do to make sure our children succeed.

Fortunately, God is always with us, whispering to our hearts, encouraging us to keep our eyes trained on the mirror of His Spirit. That's a reflection we can always count on, one in which we can see ourselves, and life, accurately.

Who are you? Who am I? These are questions we may wrestle with throughout the course of our lives. But the answers lie in who we are in Christ. In Him we are complete. We never have to look elsewhere.

§

Lord, I can never run away from You or disguise my true character. You not only see my outer image, You also see my inner heart. Never let me fail to admit my motives and see myself honestly. May I always seek Your ways and reflect Your character in everything I do so You will be glorified and well pleased.

What strength do I have, that I should still hope?
What prospects, that I should be patient? . . . I know that
you can do all things; no plan of Yours can be thwarted."
JOB 6:11; 42:2

If it were not for hope the heart would break.

AN UNEXPECTED
PHONE CALL

IT SEEMED SANDY HAD PRAYED FOR A MIRACLE NON-STOP OVER THE PAST SIX MONTHS. Everyone in her family was praying too. Still, Sandy and her husband, Rob, were unable to conceive. Since she was a little girl, all Sandy had ever wanted was to be a wife and mother. She dreamed of six children—three girls and three boys. Now it looked like she couldn't even have one.

Sandy struggled in an effort not to become angry with God, but she was still determined. Finally, she sought the help of a fertility specialist who recommended an extreme, and very expensive, procedure. Sandy agreed—she would do anything for a baby!

On the day of her appointment, Sandy was headed out the door for the clinic when the phone rang. Her younger sister, Michelle, was on the other end. Sandy quickly told Michelle that she was running late and didn't have time to talk. She was about to hang up when Michelle blurted, "Sandy, wait. You're pregnant."

"What are talking about?" Sandy responded impatiently.

"I had a dream—you're pregnant. I believe God told me."

There was something about Michelle's tone that made Sandy stop. "Are you sure?" Then Sandy felt a strong sense that God was standing right next to her.

"God told me," Michelle repeated, and Sandy believed her.

Although she was already late, Sandy went to the bathroom and rummaged through the cabinet for a home pregnancy test. (She had spent a fortune on pregnancy tests over the past several months.) One last time, she took the test.

Ten minutes later, when she called to cancel her appointment at the fertility clinic, Sandy could barely speak. She was crying for joy.

Miracles are as much a part of life today as ever. Sometimes we fail to see them in the ordinary because we've lost our ability to hope or to trust God to meet our needs or to know our desires. Try a fresh outlook toward life and expect miracles in the least likely places.

§

When I have given up hope, Lord, may I never give up on You—the source of all hope. Thank You for those beautiful surprises that remind me You are still in control of my life. And thank You for the people and circumstances that confirm Your sovereignty and Your grace.

He loads the clouds with moisture;
he scatters his lightening through them.
Now no one can look at the sun, bright as it is
in the skies after the wind has swept them clean. . . .
God comes in awesome majesty.
JOB 37:11, 21-22

Nature is but a name for an effect whose cause is God.

PERFECT CAMPING WEATHER

DONNA MILLER HAD PLANNED THIS CAMPING TRIP
FOREVER—AND BOY, DID HER FAMILY NEED IT! With two
teenagers and a husband often away on business, Donna felt like she
hardly knew them anymore. She couldn't wait to pack up the Subaru
and head for the mountain campsite they hadn't visited in years.

When the first raindrop fell on the windshield as they pulled out of
the driveway, Donna's disappointment was visible. As they drove on, the
weather became worse, and by the time they arrived at the national forest ranger station, it was a full-blown gully washer. Ron suggested that
they turn around and try it another weekend. "No," Donna said. "It will
be okay—I just know it."

Miraculously, by the time the Millers reached their campsite, the
clouds had lifted and the sun was shining on a beautiful summer day. As
Donna expected, the weekend was glorious. Her family had a blast

together fishing, hiking, roasting marshmallows, and reading the Bible by lantern light.

On Sunday afternoon, as the Millers drove away from the campsite, clouds suddenly returned and the rain began to pour. When they stopped at the forest station to check out, the ranger said, "Too bad the weather didn't cooperate this weekend."

"What do you mean? The weather was great!" Ron responded.

The ranger just looked at him with disbelief. Suddenly, Donna realized that God had parted the clouds for her family, giving them the perfect weekend. *Wow! Thank you, God. You truly are awesome,* she thought.

We often forget every storm and season is subject to God's purposes. So when weather changes, we may fail to see God's hand in it. He loves us and He gives to us what we need just when we need it, including those timely silver linings filled with His personal touch in our lives.

❧

Lord, forgive me when I doubt that You are the One who calms the raging storms of life. Sometimes I believe I have to do everything myself, though I know I am weak and weary. Like the reassurance that comes with each new dawn, Your presence renews my soul with peace and joy.

I am the Vine, you are the branches.
When you're joined with me and I with you,
the relation intimate and organic, the harvest is sure to be abundant.
Separated, you can't produce a thing.
JOHN 15:5 MSG

God is full of compassion, and never fails those who are afflicted and despised, if they trust in Him alone.

PROCESSING FAITH

PHOTOSYNTHESIS IS A BIG WORD FOR A NATURAL, EVERYDAY PROCESS. During photosynthesis, leaves use the energy from light to process water and nutrients from the soil. As the nutrients are processed, or used up, a kind of suction occurs that draws more of them up from the roots, through the branches, and into the leaves. As more nutrients are used, more are delivered.

The same could be said about your faith. God, the source of faith, serves as your nurturing "Branch." Throughout each day, there are many opportunities for you to use or process your faith. You do that each time you trust God to protect your children as they head out the door, when you reach out to others in need, or when you seek and follow His will in the myriad of daily choices that confront you.

Like leaves, you don't ever have to worry that your faith will be used up. There is a constant, steady supply available from the "Branch." The key is to stay firmly attached to the Source! To ensure that your faith supply never ends, you must continue to grow in your relationship with God. You must pray, read, study His Word, and seek His guidance for every decision in life—even the little ones. He promises that He'll be right there with His hand on your shoulder, supplying all the faith you need—and more!

By faith in Jesus Christ you are saved and by faith you have the assurance God will sustain you as you seek Him through His Word. Such faith enabled young David to confront and defeat the Philistine giant Goliath. It's faith that sets you free from personal doubts and anxiety. Tap into the Source and discover what your faith will do!

§

Lord, when my faith is weak, You are strong. You are bigger than any obstacle in my path. Help me to see You more clearly so my faith will grow, and I, like the faithful men and women who put their trust in You, will accomplish the purpose You have established for Your Kingdom through my life.

Never pay back evil for evil to anyone.
Do things in such a way that everyone can see you are honorable.
ROMANS 12:17 NLT

Be kind; everyone you meet is fighting a hard battle.

THE PATIENT
IN 315

"I'M A VOLUNTEER. I DON'T HAVE TO PUT UP WITH THIS," BRENDA SAID TO JEAN, THE HOSPITAL'S VOLUNTEER COORDINATOR. "Please don't quit," Jean begged. "Two other volunteers have already resigned this week."

The reason for the revolt among Memorial Hospital's volunteers was simple—Mr. Larsen in room 315. He was without a doubt the crankiest patient. He griped about everything—his bed was uncomfortable, his meal was cold, the doctor was always late, and the nurses were incompetent.

Brenda sighed and agreed to stay. But when it was her turn to take the magazine cart around to the patients' rooms, she regretted her decision. Standing nervously outside room 315, she took a deep breath and said a quick prayer. "Lord, help me be a help to this man as only You can be." A gentleness filled her heart. When she opened the door, she heard a gruff "What do you want?"

"Hi, Mr. Larsen, would you like a . . ." Brenda started. Suddenly, she stopped. Something inside prompted her, and without knowing why, she said, "I mean, I just want to say, I'm sorry about your wife." Startled, Mr. Larsen was speechless. He looked down and began to cry softly.

Brenda had no idea that the reason Mr. Larsen was in the hospital was that he had been in a car accident—an accident that killed his wife. Through his tears, Mr. Larsen related the tragic story to Brenda, and afterward, she offered to pray with him. Before she left, he apologized for having been such a bad patient. "It's OK," she responded. "I look forward to seeing you tomorrow." And she really meant it.

It's easy to sum up someone without really knowing all the facts. Unfortunately, we do it a lot and that equates to misjudgment. Making time and risking rejection, however, can reveal things that allow our thinking to change and our hearts to open to others. Miraculously, that's where genuine compassion begins.

§

God, I realize it's easier to take the wider path, leaving the lost, the hurt, and the lonely to find their way alone. But You want me to choose Your path, the one that forces me to notice people; and asks me to help them along the way. May I choose wisely and learn to see others as You do: as special.

The seed in the good soil, these are the ones
who have heard the word in an honest and good heart,
and hold it fast, and bear fruit with perseverance.
LUKE 8:15 NASB

Honesty is the first chapter of the book of wisdom.

ON-THE-JOB
FAITH

FINALLY, RHONDA THOUGHT AS SHE DROVE TO THE
OFFICE FOR HER FIRST DAY OF WORK. *I've made it! I am a career
woman!* A recent college graduate, she had landed a job in the accounting department of a prestigious company. Rhonda prayed as she drove,
*God, I want to be the best employee ever. Please help me honor You in my
job.*

During her first week, Rhonda joined some other employees for
lunch at which the main course was another employee. As lunch went
on, the gossip grew vicious, and although Rhonda really wanted to fit in,
she couldn't ignore God's prompting in her heart to leave.

The next week, she was tempted to follow others' example of putting
office supplies in their briefcases and "accidentally" taking them home.
Again, God's voice told her to resist joining in. *Boy,* she thought, *the
hardest part of a career has nothing to do with the work.*

Finally, when she made a mistake that cost the company money,

Rhonda thought about trying to hide it. Instead, she gathered up her courage, marched into her boss's office, and confessed.

"Fortunately, Rhonda, this mistake isn't fatal. I think we can easily make up the loss next quarter." Her boss continued, "In fact, your honesty is impressive—and rare. If you keep it up, you'll go far in this company!"

Rhonda was shocked to find that confessing a mistake actually resulted in a compliment! She was so glad that despite some pretty strong temptations, God was right there with her, helping her do the right thing.

Compromise is an insidious deceiver. Without really thinking about it, we fall prey to little lies, petty theft, and silly gossip. We may not see the harm at first, but our values and our character are compromised to God's Truth. In His Word, God reveals His desire for our lives. Let's do the right thing in the little things so it may go well with us in all things.

§

Lord, help me to recognize sin for what it is, no matter how big or how small. May I always seek You before I do or say anything that is not pleasing and acceptable to You.

Great are the works of the Lord;
they are pondered by all who delight in them.
PSALM 111:2

A thing of beauty is a joy forever.

A TALE OF FLOWERS AND BUGS

IT WAS TRUE THAT MELODY PUSHED HER DAUGHTER, BUT SHE KNEW THAT IF LIBBY HAD THE OPPORTUNITY, SHE COULD REALLY SHINE. In fact, from the time she was a baby, Libby was in one beauty contest after another. She had won the Baby Beautiful contest when she was only three months old.

Now that Libby was five, Melody had set her sights on the Little Miss Carson County pageant and endlessly drilled her reluctant daughter in the finer points of standing up straight, smiling continually, and providing the right answers to judges' questions.

One summer afternoon, Melody asked Libby to gather flowers from the garden for the dining table. She had invited a pageant judge to dinner and wanted everything to be perfect. When Libby returned from the garden, she carried not only a bouquet of daisies but also a pocketful of ladybugs, caterpillars, and roly-polys.

"Mommy, look at what I brought to go on the flowers," Libby said as she started to take her stash of bugs out of her pocket.

Horrified, Melody told Libby to "get those things out of here." Libby responded, "But, Mommy, God doesn't just love the flowers. He loves the bugs, too."

Melody was amazed by the wisdom of her daughter's words, feeling they were a direct message to her from God. As she finished preparing for dinner, she was glad she would have the opportunity to tell the pageant judge in person that Libby wouldn't be a contestant in the upcoming pageant after all.

God sees beauty all around us, in everything great and small. The tragedy is when we fail to acknowledge it and the One who created it. Relish all the moments and people in your life every day. God does.

§

In every season and in every day, Lord, You provide us with opportunities to marvel at Your beautiful creation. Thank You for eyes to see just how beautiful You are, even when we aren't looking.

Charm is deceptive, and beauty is fleeting;
but a woman who fears the Lord is to be praised.
PROVERBS 31:30

A man's good work is affected by doing
what he does; a woman's by being what she is.

HEATHER'S BIG NEWS

Prom, homecoming, and formal banquets. Since Heather was born, Mary had looked forward to shopping with her daughter for the perfect dress, putting her hair up in ringlets, and taking photos when her date picked her up for that special event.

The problem was, Heather wasn't cooperative. She was a senior, and she hadn't been to even one banquet or homecoming dance. Instead, Heather spent Friday nights hanging out with the youth group at Pizza Palace. The most she ever got dressed up was a peasant skirt and flip-flops, and Mary despaired that she would never see her daughter trade in her pigtails for ringlets.

Lately, however, there was a glimmer of hope. Heather had begun to spend time with Paul, a cute boy from algebra class. He often came over for study sessions and had gone with Heather to a couple of youth group meetings.

Then it happened—the day Mary had waited for. A breathless

Heather came rushing into the kitchen. "Mom, you'll never guess what Paul just asked me!" Mary thanked God—prom was coming up, and she was so grateful her daughter was finally going.

"What did he ask you, honey?"

"He asked me how to be saved!"

Suddenly, Mary felt God's hand on her shoulder as if to say, *This is where your focus should be.* Of course, Heather had it right all along. Evening gowns and perfume had their place, but they paled in the light of a young boy's need for salvation. "Heather, I'm so proud of you," Mary said.

As mothers, you may want to micro-manage your children's lives and choices, especially with the many things that tempt us in our "have-it-all-now" culture, but we need to resist the temptation. With prayer and God's mercy, you can give your children the opportunity to make good choices.

§

Lord, help me to remember that no matter how much I love my children, You love them more, and You are protecting them. They are Yours. Help me be the best parent I can be and not get in the way of Your purposes.

"If you believe, you will receive whatever you ask for in prayer."
MATTHEW 21:22 NLT

Faith declares what the senses do not see.

GOD'S PERFECT HEALING

THE X-RAYS WERE THE SAME—NO NEW BONE GROWTH.
After six weeks of rehabilitation, the breaks in Mrs. Rayburn's legs were just as pronounced as they were the day she arrived. She had survived a crippling case of polio in her teens, and lived a normal life with three children and a career as a junior high teacher. She had always been a little unsteady on her feet and had often suffered broken bones from sudden falls, but she was used to that.

It was different this time. Adding advanced osteoporosis to a fall that severely fractured both legs, the prognosis was not good for the now seventy-year-old woman. Each week, the doctor searched her X-rays for even the smallest sign of new bone. There was none. Any other patient would have resigned herself to the evidence of the X-rays. But Mrs. Rayburn said, confidently, "God is always with me. He didn't bring me this far only to have me spend the rest of my life in a wheelchair."

While Mrs. Rayburn remained in the hospital, her family prepared for the worst. Her husband looked into full-time nursing assistance, and her grown children prayed they would know how to help in the face of tragedy.

Then in the seventh week, there was the tiniest, almost undetectable sign of fuzziness on Mrs. Rayburn's X-ray. The doctor almost cried at the sight. But Mrs. Rayburn just smiled and said, "Told you so." She added, "I'll miss the hospital. I don't often have the chance to get caught up on my reading."

Even when chances don't look good, miracles happen. God is more reliable than mere chances. Sometimes He allows us to do all we can, and then He steps forward and brings about His perfect design for our lives. Never give up hope. God is always at work!

§

Lord, forgive me when I doubt Your ability to hear and to answer my prayer. Thank you for the beautiful people You put in my life who exemplify simple faith—even the faith of a mustard seed. With faith, all things are possible.

Keep your eye on what you're doing;
accept the hard times along with the good; keep the Message alive;
do a thorough job as God's servant.
2 TIMOTHY 4:5 MSG

Hard work is a thrill and a joy when you are in the will of God.

JOB #1

TEACHER, HOMEMAKER, DOCTOR, SALES CLERK—
WOMEN TODAY HAVE MORE CAREER OPTIONS THAN EVER.
Unfortunately, our society says some jobs are worth more than others,
implying that some people are more important than others. Think about
it. The typical company CEO could be gone for a month, and few
would even notice their absence. But if the janitorial crew didn't show
up one day, it could mean company-wide disaster. Trash cans could over-
flow, bathroom paper towel dispensers could go empty, coffee urns could
sit with cold, stale coffee.

Who's job is more important?

While we're quick to believe one job is better than another, Jesus says
that what we do from 9 to 5, Monday through Friday, is really second-
ary to the job He's given us—to be a living witness for Him. Our number one job is ministry whether we work with children in a kindergarten
classroom, seniors in a retirement center, or other adults in the world of
office cubicles. Consider the apostle Paul, for example. He was a tent-
maker by trade, but we don't know him today because of his tent-mak-

ing career. We know him because he dedicated his life to ministry and to others. If you look around, you'll see countless ways every day to minister to those in your work environment. And if you ask God, who is always only a prayer away, He will help you share with them the wonderful difference that His presence can make in their lives.

God wants us to be good teachers, homemakers, doctors, and sales clerks. But, even more importantly, He wants us to excel at our primary job—ministry!

Somewhere we've gotten off course, thinking we are what we do instead of whose we are. As Christians, our identity must be in Christ, alone. And our mission is to live out His love through the many aspects of our lives—including our careers, no matter how lofty or how humble.

§

Forgive me, Father, when I become carried away with my own importance or whenever I fail to appreciate the value of a job well done, despite its lack of prestige. May all I do be a love offering to You, poured out for Your Kingdom and for Your service.

His lord said to him, "Well done, good and faithful servant;
you were faithful over a few things, I will make you ruler
over many things. Enter into the joy of your lord."
MATTHEW 25:21 NKJV

One on God's side is a majority.

A CLUB WORTHY
OF MEMBERSHIP

THE VOTE WAS IN; JANELLE WAS OUT—OF THE GARDEN CLUB, THAT IS. It was the most exclusive club in town, and when she applied, Janelle had the best garden in the neighborhood. But she soon found that a stunning garden wasn't as important as "other factors" to the club. After the devastating news, she asked her friend Bonnie, a long-standing member, why she wasn't voted in.

Bonnie confided to Janelle, "Frankly, the other women didn't think you would fit in because you talk a lot about Jesus." Janelle recalled that she had said she would be unable to attend functions on Thursday evenings—her Bible study night.

Janelle still felt pangs of rejection the next Sunday when a preacher from China spoke at church. He told the congregation that the Chinese authorities constantly harassed him for preaching the gospel. At one point, he had been imprisoned for three years, and suffered regular beatings—some so severe he was taken to the hospital and once slipped into a coma. Yet when he was released from prison, he went right back to preaching. He said, "No law or persecution will ever stop me from telling people about Jesus Christ."

As she listened to the sufferings of this brave man, Janelle no longer felt bad about rejection by the Garden Club. In fact, she felt God's blessing flow into her heart for suffering rejection in His name. She felt Him whisper in her ear, *Well done, good and faithful servant.*

Jesus said that in this world you would be persecuted for His name's sake. But He also said He would never leave you or forsake you. When you feel persecuted for your faith, don't look down on yourself, look around. You will find yourself in some very good company!

§

Lord, You know firsthand how bad rejection feels. But You overcame rejection—as well as death. As Your child, You have empowered me to do the same. Thanks to Your love, I can endure the initial pain of every worldly let-down because I anticipate the joy of a life spent with You forever.

God said, "Let there be light"; and there was light.
GENESIS 1:3 NASB

All miracles are simply feeble lights
like beacons on our way to the port where shines the light,
the total light of the resurrection.

A LIGHT IN
THE STORM

USUALLY, SUE AND HER CHILDREN LIKED THUNDER-
STORMS. It was fun to guess how far away the lightning was by count-
ing the seconds between the flash and the thunder. The rain spatter on
the windows was like a tickle from God, and the house felt warm and
cozy inside. But this time, the storm wasn't fun, and the feelings weren't
warm or cozy.

It hit in the middle of the night with frightening force. There were
no seconds to count between the blinding flashes of lightning and deaf-
ening thunder claps. Sheets of rain and golf-ball-sized hail pounded the
windows. Not long after the storm started, all three kids and the dog ran
down the hall and dove into Sue's bed. Dan was out of town on business, and Sue had to admit that even she was afraid.

The group huddled together, and then suddenly the lights went out.
Sue began to panic when she remembered that there was a flashlight in
the nightstand. She pulled it out and turned it on. Immediately, its little spot of light spread a feeling of comfort and security over the room.

Sue felt God's presence in the light and His assurance that everything would be all right.

Soon after, the storm let up and Sue, the kids, and the dog drifted off to sleep. The next morning, when she returned the flashlight to the nightstand, she noticed for the first time that it felt unusually light. Curious, she unscrewed the end, and was amazed to find there were no batteries inside.

You may not recognize God's everyday miracles in your life, until a storm comes. When fears surface you have the opportunity to stretch your faith. In trying circumstances, God's miraculous power remains constant and true, providing you with what you need just when you need it. Never doubt it.

§

*Lord, Your Word is a lamp for my feet and a light on my path . . .
may I never walk in darkness. Thank You for being the Light in my
life at all times, in good times and bad. May I praise Your name and
proclaim Your kindness without ceasing.*

*To go after God . . . to do good, to be rich
in helping others, to be extravagantly generous.
If they do that, they'll build a treasury that
will last, gaining life that is truly life.*
1 TIMOTHY 6:17-19 MSG

To profit from good advice requires more wisdom than to give it.

THE BEST
INVESTMENT
ADVICE

THERE ARE FEW PEOPLE IN THE WORLD WHOSE WORDS
WIELD MORE POWER THAN ALAN GREENSPAN, CHAIRMAN
OF THE FEDERAL RESERVE BOARD. A few years ago, in a quick,
ten-sentence statement made at a dinner given by the American
Enterprise Institute, Greenspan shook financial markets around the
world. Less than an hour after his statement, the stock market in
Australia took a nosedive. Following suit, the Japanese and German markets tumbled, and the Dow-Jones industrial average lost more than 144
points.

Obviously, when Greenspan talks, investors listen. In the same way,
when God speaks to our hearts we should listen, because He is the expert
about the things we have invested our lives into. Sometimes He prompts

us to take drastic action, to "invest our resources" in different ways. For example, when we're in a relationship that does not honor Him, He will often direct us to end that relationship and invest in other, more positive relationships.

Other times, God directs us to sit tight, be patient, and wait for Him to work. We may, for instance, be desperate to get out of a miserable job, but for some reason, nothing else seems to open up. It might be that God is saying, *Wait. I have a different plan that will be so much better for you!*

God knows what's best for us, and we should stay tuned to His will for the investment of our resources—our love, our time, our talents, and even our money.

The best way to fully understand God's desire for you is to remain in constant communication with Him through prayer. With such a relationship, you can rest assured He will orchestrate the circumstances that honor your patience and diligence. Wait upon the Lord and expect wonderful blessings.

$

Lord, I need You in my life and in my future. I trust You to know what is best for me. Grant me the wisdom to wait, listen, and act as You lead.

He will not let your foot slip—
he who watches over you will not slumber; indeed,
he who watches over Israel will neither slumber nor sleep.
PSALM 121:3-4

Do not fail one another in interest, care,
and practical help; but mostly do not fail one another in prayer.

ROBIN'S
MIDNIGHT
WALK

IT WAS ROBIN'S FIRST TRIP TO NEW YORK. She was scheduled to attend a professional training conference in Manhattan. Robin was more excited about seeing the sights than the conference. Before she decided which workshops to attend, she decided which Broadway shows she would see in the evenings.

The evening she saw Cats, she walked to the theater. It was only a few blocks from her hotel. Afterward, she strolled out of the theater, humming a medley of Cats tunes. Two blocks later, Robin suddenly realized that the street was dark, and scary. She glanced at her watch—11:00 P.M. Fear grew as she passed shadowy figures lounging in doorways. One said something to her that she couldn't quite make out. She picked up her pace, clutched her purse tightly, and began to hum a Scripture song.

Immediately, a strong assurance that God was right there with her filled her heart, and it wasn't long before she was in the brightly lit lobby of her hotel.

Later, relating her adventure to her Bible study group back home, Christine asked, "What day and time did you say that was?"

"It was on Wednesday, about eleven o'clock."

"That's eight our time." The four other group members exchanged looks of amazement.

"What? What's up?" Robin asked.

Christine explained, "On Wednesday at eight o'clock, I had a strong feeling to pray for you. I called everyone in the group, and we were praying for you—at the exact time you walked back to the hotel."

"Wow!" the whole group said in unison.

God desires that you not only bring your own praises and requests to Him, but that you also remember the needs of others. Intercessory prayer is powerful. Pray for someone today!

༄

Lord, I realize You already know my deepest needs and my times of despair. Yet, You also want me to bring them before Your throne of grace in an act of faith and obedience. Thank you for answered prayer.

Your dwelling place is secure, your nest is set in a rock.
NUMBERS 24:21

Happiness is found only in the home where
God is loved and honored, where each one loves and
helps and cares for the others.

MY PERFECT
HOUSE

STEPHANIE WAS HAPPY. Her husband's company had opened
an office in Pennsylvania, and Bill was asked to manage the new facility.
She was also sad because she had lived in Glendale for the past 20 years.
Her children had grown up there, all her friends were there, and she
loved the Glendale Community Church, where she and Bill were faithful members.

The day the real estate agent picked up she and Bill at the hotel in
Pennsylvania to hunt for houses was difficult. But she put on a happy
face and made small talk as the agent took them from house to house.
Nothing struck Stephanie as the right place.

Finally, the agent said there was one more house on her list. Bill and
Stephanie were both relieved. The car had barely stopped in front of the
house on Maple Street when Stephanie enthusiastically bolted out the
door saying, "This is it. This is the one."

Back at the hotel, Bill asked Stephanie why she was so enthusiastic about the Maple Street house when she had liked nothing else the rest of the day. She explained that when she and her sisters were little, they played a game called "My Perfect House," for which they would describe what their dream house would look like. Amazingly, the Maple Street house was exactly the one she pictured as "perfect" each time they played the game.

Bill and Stephanie held hands and prayed, thanking God for showing them without a doubt that He was with them in their move. A new excitement was deposited in Stephanie that day. She would miss her friends but looked forward to her new adventure with Bill—and God.

Your heavenly Father is pleased to honor your dreams and special desires when you give them back to Him. Doing so requires trust—a trust that believes the outcome is God's best for you no matter what, and a trust that avoids the temptation of self-sufficiency. Seek the courage to trust God's ways and discover the very best He has for you in the process!

ॐ

Lord, thank You for answered prayers—even when those answers differ from what I may have asked or desired. Thank You for loving me so much that even my dreams and desires are important to You.

As Elijah stood there, the Lord passed by, . . .
but the Lord was not in the wind. . . .
the Lord was not in the earthquake. . . .
the Lord was not in the fire.
And after the fire there was the sound of a gentle whisper.
When Elijah heard it, he wrapped his face in his cloak.
1 KINGS 19:11-13 NLT

**Communication is something so simple
and difficult that we can never put it in simple words.**

HELLO!
ANYONE
THERE?

COMMUNICATION DEVICES CONTINUE TO BECOME
MORE AND MORE SOPHISTICATED. Now we communicate by
wireless phones that are smaller than a deck of cards yet can send and
receive photos. When we're online, we can "instant message" each other.
And how did we ever manage without e-mail?

Throughout history, God used some pretty innovative ways to communicate with people too. He sent seven plagues, including a whopper
of a hailstorm and hordes of locusts, to tell Pharaoh to free the Israelites
from captivity in Egypt. He sent a shepherd boy to kill a giant with the

message that God's people would not be defeated. He sent an angel to tell Mary that she was pregnant with His Son.

The Bible is full of spectacular communications from God. But what about today? How does God keep in touch with us?

He still chooses spectacular ways to communicate. The news often reports miraculous events that can only be explained as divine intervention. But more often, He communicates in quiet, everyday ways—through the advice of a friend, through the unexpected words of wisdom that come from your children's mouths, through that unshakeable feeling in your heart, or that sudden "Why didn't I think of that before?" idea that pops into your mind.

In fact, God communicates with you all the time, but you have to listen closely and keep the lines open. Listening keeps His messages from becoming lost in the static of your life.

How does God speak today? In the everyday things of life and through the people around us, God reveals Himself and His message of love in creative and gentle ways. You may need to slow down, be quiet, and listen. He is only a breath away.

§

Father, the unheard sound of Your presence gives me great peace, joy, and assurance. Help me each day to be still enough to hear You and to share my thoughts with You. Through this intimate communication process, I know I will grow in relationship and communion with You.

He shall give His angels charge over you,
to keep you in all your ways.
PSALM 91:11 NKJV

The servants of Christ are protected by invisible,
rather than visible, beings. But if these guard you,
they do so because they have been summoned by your prayers.

ANGELS
WATCHING
OVER ME

SHERRY BAKER WAS STUMPED. The girls in her Sunday School class asked the kinds of questions that second-graders are famous for.

"Is it true I have a guardian angel?"

"Is my angel a boy or a girl?"

"Does my kitty have an angel?"

"If I have an angel, how come I broke my arm last summer?"

Sherry answered them, "If the Bible says God sends His angels to watch over us, then it must be true." But she had to admit in her heart she wasn't sure. She had seen TV shows about angels rushing in at the last second to snatch people from impending doom. It was good entertainment, but Sherry suspected the whole guardian angel thing was just that—Hollywood.

That is, until she received a call from a church friend. A car had struck Emily, one of her Sunday School students. Sherry grabbed her purse and immediately left for the hospital. When she arrived, she overhead the doctor tell Emily's parents, "It's amazing. The force that hit Emily should have killed her, but she was just knocked cold. Since she's been here, we've conducted every test and there's nothing—no broken bones, no internal bleeding, nothing."

Sherry felt God whisper to her, *Now do you believe?* She still had her doubts until she actually saw Emily, sitting up in her hospital bed, merrily chattering away. "How do you feel, Emily?"

"I feel fine, Mrs. Baker. And guess what—I think my angel's a girl!"

Even when it's difficult to believe, God provides opportunities to help us in our disbelief. Throughout His Word, God teaches us about the role of angels and how they serve Him to convey messages, provide protection, and orchestrate miracles. Rediscover the faith of a child. Appreciate the work of God's special messengers.

§

God, I experience times of disbelief. Help me to renew the faith I knew as a child. Thank You for using special angels to minister to me and to others. May I always acknowledge and praise You for Your abiding mercy and love.

Honor your father and your mother,
that your days may be long upon the land
which the Lord your God is giving you.
EXODUS 20:12 NKJV

The wisest thing is Time, for it brings everything to light.

TOUGH DECISIONS, GOOD DECISIONS

MOVING HER MOTHER INTO A RETIREMENT HOME WAS HARD FOR ELISE. She was particularly sad the day her mom's house sold. Elise and her brother, Frank, had grown up there, and it was filled with special memories. She and Frank prayed for God's guidance, and they both felt His blessing on their decision. But when moving day came, Elise felt sick at heart. God, are you sure this is the right thing to do?

The first day Elise went to visit her mom after the move she was surprised to find that the 80-year-old woman was not in her room. Anxious, Elise went in search of her mother.

She found her in the recreation room, playing bridge. "I'll be just a minute, dear," her mom said without taking her eyes off her cards. Elise read a magazine while the game went on—and on. Finally, she interrupted, "I've got to go, Mom. I'll come back when we can spend time together."

"I'm so sorry, honey. Come back soon. We'll have a nice, long chat."

On her way to the car she felt at peace with their decision. It was as if God gently patted her shoulder to say, *I told you this was the right way.*

Elise learned that a "nice, long chat" with her mother meant she had to call ahead and reserve a place on her busy schedule. Usually, that was on Thursdays between square dancing lessons and dinner.

Elise hadn't seen her mother so happy since her father died. After one Thursday visit, she chuckled at the thought of her mother, the social butterfly, and thanked God for helping her and Frank make the best decision for their mother.

The passage of time is inevitable, and with it comes both change and responsibility. Time and the impact it has on our life or that of others is nothing to fear. Take the difficult decisions to God and allow Him to show you what to do. Then you will know peace.

§

Lord, it is easy to feel overwhelmed with important life decisions.
Yet You tell us in Your Word to bring our concerns to You
for Your yoke is easy and Your burden is light. Help me to trust
You with all my decisions.

How do you benefit if you gain the whole world
but lose your own soul in the process?
Is anything worth more than your soul?
MATTHEW 16:26 NLT

Try not to become a person of success
but rather try to become a person of value.

SUCCESS IN GOD'S EYES

THE PHRASE "THE SWEET SMELL OF SUCCESS" IS A POP-
ULAR ONE, JUST AS THE PURSUIT OF SUCCESS IS AN
ACCEPTED PART OF AMERICAN LIFE. Success means different
things to different women, depending on the "smell" they seek. For
some, the smell of a baby means success. For others, the smell of a
brand-new car speaks success. Some women consider the smell of a
newly painted corner office with big windows to be the "sweet smell of
success." Children, material things, prestige, and power are just a few of
the things American women pursue.

Interestingly, according to a survey conducted by the Barna Research
Group, 51 percent of Christians believe money is the primary symbol of
success, and 19 percent say you can tell how successful someone is by
looking at what they own. But the refreshing truth is, God doesn't meas-
ure your success by whether or not you have children, what the sticker

price on your car is, or whether you stand on the corporate ladder.

The "sweet smell of success" to God is a woman who seeks Him with her whole heart—a woman like Mary, who was not exactly the epitome of success by Nazareth standards, but was considered worthy to be the mother of God's only Son.

Or what about Esther, who made what would be termed today an "extreme career limiting move" to stand up for her people and her Lord?

These women are successful in God's eyes. They cultivated a close relationship with Him and were ready to follow His will, knowing that He would always be close by, guiding them to success. They are the kind of women we need to focus on as examples of true success.

Looks can be deceiving. Invest in what's inside your heart and soul instead of what's on your body or in your life. The only image of success that matters is the one God sees and approves.

§

Lord, sometimes I get caught up in the world's idea of success instead of focusing on Your purpose for my life. Give me eyes for the things You value: a loving heart and a compassionate spirit.

All this newness of life is from God, who brought us
back to himself through what Christ did.
And God has given us the task of reconciling people to him.
2 CORINTHIANS 5:18 NLT

If it were not for hope the heart would break.

AN INFANT'S GIFT

JOANNE HADN'T SEEN HER DAUGHTER KATIE SINCE
AUGUST 5, 1997, THE DAY THE 19-YEAR-OLD ANNOUNCED
SHE HAD QUIT COLLEGE TO LIVE IN PARIS WITH HER
BOYFRIEND. The ensuing argument was one for the record books and
ended when Katie stomped out the door, and vowed never to see her
mother again.

Now, Joanne kept up with her daughter through friends who occa-
sionally called her to update her on Katie's whereabouts. Although she
never had the courage to try to contact Katie, Joanne prayed for her every
day. Over time, Joanne learned much about intercessory prayer. She
prayed for everything in Katie's life . . . her relationships, her physical
health, her spiritual well-being, her finances, and her happiness. Mostly
she prayed God would bring something or someone into her daughter's
life that would persuade her to restore their relationship. Often she would
experience a calm assurance that someday that would happen.

Then one afternoon there was a knock at Joanne's door. She looked though the peephole to see Katie with a baby in her arms. When she opened the door, the two fell into each other's arms and didn't let go until the baby, caught between them, began to cry.

Katie introduced Joanne to her granddaughter. Joanne was overjoyed. As they caught up with each other's lives over a pitcher of iced tea, Joanne worked up the courage to say, "Why did you decide to come back?"

Katie said, "After Hannah was born, I knew you were praying for me because each time I looked into her face I heard God speak to my heart. He told me you love me as much as I love Hannah!"

As Joanne held her sleeping granddaughter, the answer to her prayer, she whispered into her tiny ear, "Thank you."

Parenting is tough. Prayer is crucial. As children develop individual personalities and seek to find their way in the world, parenting takes on dimensions few feel prepared to fully handle. Despite relational problems, hope remains. Keep a light on for the prodigal in all of us.

§

God, You use everything and everyone to fulfill Your purposes—even the least among us. As the God of reconciliation, You never give up on us, and You remind us to never give up on each other.

Stand firm then, with the belt of truth
buckled around your waist, with the breastplate
of righteousness in place, and with your feet fitted
with the readiness that comes from the gospel of peace.
EPHESIANS 6:14-15

Always vote for a principle, though you vote alone, and you may
cherish the sweet reflection that your vote is never lost.

STANDING UP TO PRESSURE

UNLIKE MOST PEOPLE, NICKI WANTED TO BE CHOSEN FOR JURY DUTY. She thought it would be fascinating to see firsthand the American justice system at work. But when she was finally chosen, Nicki had second thoughts. It was a high-profile murder trial likely to last for several weeks. Nevertheless, Nicki believed it was her duty to serve, and was determined to be a conscientious juror no matter how long the trial went.

In the jury box, Nicki paid close attention to all the evidence. She went over her notes every evening, taking seriously her responsibility to make the right decision.

Nicki was surprised when the jury took its first vote after the trial ended. All but one of the jurors voted "guilty." As the only holdout, she was amazed everyone else thought the defendant was guilty. But Nicki knew in her heart he was innocent, and for the next three days, she stood alone against the other jurors, explaining why.

Generally a person who didn't like to make waves, Nicki often thought about giving up, but God prompted her, *Be strong. I'll help you.*

After three days, it was clear Nicki wasn't about to budge—neither were the other jurors. A mistrial was declared and a new trial set.

One morning before the new trial date arrived, Nicki picked up the newspaper to read that the real murderer had confessed. She thanked God for giving her the strength to do the right thing, and further read that the man she had known was innocent all along had been released.

Not only is it difficult to stand up for what you believe is right, it is difficult to discern what is right. Avoid easy answers. Seek the truth, pray for direction, stand for your convictions, and trust God with the results.

෮

I want to do the right thing and make the right decisions. But I cannot do it without involving You, God. Keep me humble so I may always feel Your leading and Your power in the decisions I make.

"The religion scholars and Pharisees are competent
teachers in God's Law. You won't go wrong
in following their teachings on Moses. But be careful
about following them. They talk a good line,
but they don't live it. They don't take it into their
hearts and live it out in their behavior."
MATTHEW 23:2-3 MSG

Solemn prayers and rapturous devotions are but repeated
hypocrisies unless the heart and mind be conformable to them.

IT'S WHAT'S INSIDE THAT COUNTS

WE ALL KNOW WHAT HAPPENS WHEN YOU SQUEEZE A
SPONGE SATURATED WITH WATER—THE WATER RUNS OUT.
The pressure, no matter how slight, causes whatever is in the sponge to
flow out.

Recently, we have seen pressure put on several big American corporations. When they were "squeezed," what flowed out was not pretty—
long-term deception and deep-seated greed. Even with elaborate cover-
ups and highly-paid lawyers, the true nature of the executives who ran
these corporations flowed out with devastating results for many innocent people.

Of all the sins that Jesus condemned, He was particularly critical of hypocrisy, or trying to pass yourself off as something you're not. Jesus often confronted the religious leaders of His day who tried to pass themselves off as pious, righteous, and better than everyone else. On several occasions, Jesus put pressure on them. When He did, their true nature flowed out. They were, in fact, self-serving, greedy, and egotistical.

At one point, Jesus compared them to tombs that appear white and clean on the outside but are filled with putrid, decaying bones on the inside. It was strong language, but it left no doubt for believers of how God views hypocrisy.

God wants us to be filled with His character—love, joy, peace, patience, kindness, goodness, faithfulness, gentleness, and self-control. The more we strive to develop His character, the more we feel His presence and love in our hearts. And if we keep Him close, we know that when life puts pressure on us, what flows out of our character will be honoring to Him.

Jesus hated the hypocrites of His day, and He hates the hypocrites of today. To avoid being a hypocrite, fill your life with the fruits of the spirit—love, joy, peace, patience, kindness, goodness, faithfulness, gentleness, and self-control.

§

Lord, it is my desire to be a person after Your own heart;
a person who seeks to serve instead of being served,
a person who loves the unlovely. Point out my hypocritical tendencies
so I may be worthy of the name "Christian."

You prepare a table before me . . . surely goodness
and love will follow me all the days of my life and I will
dwell in the house of the Lord forever.
PSALM 23:5-6

Hospitality is one form of worship.

A PLACE AT
THE TABLE

IT HAD BEEN TWO YEARS SINCE HER HUSBAND'S DEATH,
AND STACEY STILL SET HIS PLACE AT THE DINNER TABLE.
She prayed that in His time, God would bring the right person to fill the
empty place. In the meantime, she had her hands full helping her two
young sons deal with their grief. Russ, age five, had trouble sleeping, and
Rob, age eight, was failing in school.

Stacey enrolled Rob in an after-school tutoring program on the
advice of her neighbor, who declared that it had turned her child from a
D to a B student. Stacey really liked Rob's tutor, Ken, and as time went
by, she found herself spending more and more time chatting with him
after Rob's sessions. They had so much in common, including their faith
in Christ, and she enjoyed Ken's easy smile and his way with children.
She wondered if God had brought Ken into her life to be more than
Rob's tutor.

Rob soon brought his grades back up, and while he was excited that he wouldn't have to go to tutoring anymore, Stacey was disappointed. The evening of Rob's last tutoring session, Stacey planned a special dinner with all his favorite foods, including a big chocolate cake. Just as she began to cut the cake, the doorbell rang. Ken was at the door. He had stopped by to return a book Rob had left at the tutoring center that afternoon. Stacey invited him in for a piece of cake.

"Oh, I don't want to interrupt," Ken said.

"No, I insist," Stacey said. "There's already a place set at the table." As she cut a piece of cake for Ken, she knew that God had, indeed, brought him to fill the empty place at her table and in her heart.

With God nothing is ironic, coincidental, or circumstantial. Everything works together for those who trust the Lord and desire His will for their lives. Anticipate beautiful things from the God who loves you.

δ

Thank You, God, for loving me so much that You intervene in the minute things of life to satisfy the desires of my heart. May I always see You in special appointments and praise Your name forever.

You can't get forgiveness from God, for instance,
without also forgiving others. If you refuse to do your part,
you cut yourself off from God's part.
MATTHEW 6:14-15 MSG

Forgiveness is one's deepest need and highest achievement.

JOURNEY TO FORGIVENESS

REBECCA HAD NOT SPOKEN TO HER FATHER SINCE SHE WAS 15 YEARS OLD. That's when he left for work on a bright June morning and never came back. Now 30 years old, Rebecca argued with God, who spoke to her heart daily, *Forgive him.* But she just couldn't do it. *Help me, God,* she thought. *The hurt is just too deep.*

A nurse at the local hospital phoned her. Her dad had suffered a heart attack, and it didn't look like he had long to live. "So?" Rebecca asked.

"He wants to see you," the nurse replied.

When she walked through the door of his hospital room, although it had been 15 years, Rebecca's dad immediately recognized her and held out his hand. Rebecca hesitantly took it. When she said, "How are you, Dad?" he began to cry. Through his tears, he asked his daughter for a favor. He wanted to be saved, but didn't know what to do. "I know I don't deserve it, but will you help me?" At that moment complete, supernatural forgiveness for him flooded through Rebecca. *Thank you, God,* she thought.

Amazingly, after Rebecca led her dad to Jesus, he immediately began to get better. His doctor was astounded at the recovery, and the day he left the hospital, he was declared by the staff to be a miracle. In fact, he went on to become a faithful and active member of Rebecca's church, forged a new relationship with his daughter, and lived another ten years.

Unforgiveness not only breaks hearts, it also destroys lives. Search your heart and seek the ability to forgive others and to seek forgiveness where there is pain. Allow spiritual healing to begin today.

❧

Lord, because You forgave me my past and my failures, empower me now to forgive others and myself. Love and peace cannot flourish where forgiveness has not yet cultivated fertile ground for relationships. Thank You for setting the perfect example of forgiveness and love.

*The one who plants and the one who waters
work as a team with the same purpose. . . .
We work together as partners who belong to God.*
1 CORINTHIANS 3:8-9 NLT

The Church is the family of God.
It is seen in miniature in each family.

THE BENEFITS OF BELONGING

WHEN SOMEONE ASKS WHERE YOU ATTEND CHURCH, IT'S COMMON TO SAY, "I BELONG TO . . . ." There's a big difference between belonging to a church and attending one. Think about uses of the word belong. You might say, "That child belongs to me" or "I belong to a really large family back east." In other words, we often use it when referring to our closest relationships.

We should also work to cultivate close, belonging relationships within our church. The apostle Paul, in his second letter to the Corinthians, compares the church to the body and each church member to a different part of the body. Just as our fingers or ears belong to our body and perform unique and important tasks, God means for each of us to belong to a church and perform unique and important tasks. And just as a foot can't do what a hand does, and vice versa, no one else can provide what you have to give to the life of your church.

When you belong to a church instead of merely attending one, it's also easier for God to provide guidance for your daily life. He often reveals His presence to you through other members. Through them, He can speak to you, showing you His wisdom and direction—just as the eyes help the feet know where to go. Those who don't belong to a church, but just attend services, are missing out on one of God's most vital sources of help and direction for life.

Jesus gave His life for the Church, and He is returning soon to take Her home to live with Him forever. Don't miss the reunion! You're a vital part of the Church, and you have an important role to play. Be there.

§

I was glad when they said to me, "Let us go into the house of the Lord" (Psalm 122:1). I love to meet You in Your house of worship, Lord. I love those who gather with me to pray and to learn of You. Thank You for the Church and its many shapes, sizes, and color variations. I long for the day when the entire Body assembles with You in heaven.

*You art my hiding place; You preserve
me from trouble; You surround me
with songs of deliverance.*
PSALM 32:7 NASB

God's help is just a prayer away.

SHELTER
FROM THE
STORM

MOST PEOPLE TOOK THE HIGHWAY BETWEEN
BLOOMINGTON AND HAYES, BUT GWEN KNEW A BACK-
ROAD SHORTCUT. She was glad that after college graduation, she
landed a teaching job at Bloomington Elementary School. It was close
to Hayes, where her parents lived, yet still far enough away to feel independent.

One Friday afternoon in January, after a long week, Gwen decided
to make a trip home for the weekend. The weather reports were posting
winter storm warnings, but Gwen didn't care—her car had four-wheel
drive.

Not long into her drive, the blizzard hit. It grew more and more difficult for Gwen to see the road, and when she misjudged a curve, her car
slid into the ditch.

Gwen waited in her stuck car for someone to drive by, but no one did. When it began to get dark, she decided to walk. To where, she didn't know. There was a farmhouse close by, but it had been deserted for years.

As night fell, Gwen began to panic. *God, help me. Send someone, please.* As she walked, her panic gave way to a warm feeling of God's protection. Finally, she saw the deserted farmhouse ahead. To her astonishment, there was a light shining on the porch. When she reached the house, a young couple answered her knock.

Warming up by the fire, Gwen explained her predicament.

"Actually," the young woman said, "we just moved in yesterday." She added with a chuckle, "Looks like we're just in time to save you from becoming an icicle!"

Remember, God is always with us, and He will assist us with whatever we need, whenever we need it, if we just trust Him.

§

God, You know I become frightened when things beyond my control happen. Help me to trust You during these situations, learning more of Your faithfulness. Thank You for being my ultimate comfort and help. Thank You for others who serve as Your outstretched arms in critical moments.

Bring all the tithes into the storehouse.
MALACHI 3:10 NKJV

If a person has a right attitude toward money,
it will help straighten out almost every other area in life.

PROVING GOD'S FAITHFULNESS

WHY NOW? THOUGHT TAMMY. SHE HAD SAT THROUGH COUNTLESS SERMONS IN HER LIFE ABOUT TITHING, BUT SHE NEVER REALLY FELT THE NEED TO GIVE A TENTH OF HER EARNINGS TO THE CHURCH. Not that she was stingy with her offerings, but a tenth always sounded like way too much.

Why now, when her husband Carl was out of work, when the family was surviving on unemployment and Tammy's earnings from teaching piano lessons—why was God impressing on her heart to tithe? Repeatedly she heard Him say, *Prove me!* as if Malachi 3:10 were just for her. When she began to lose sleep because of her growing conviction about tithing, she brought the subject up with Carl.

Surprisingly, Carl had felt the same tug at his heart to give a tenth of whatever they earned back to God. When they wrote out a check, Tammy and Carl felt good about their decision but the next Sunday, when the offering plate came to them, they hesitated. Tammy took a big breath as she heard a gentle whisper seemingly from over her shoulder,

Prove me! She dropped the check into the plate and quickly passed it on.

The next day, Carl checked the mail, and came running back into the house. "Tammy! You're not going to believe it! I totally forgot that I lent Tony some money last year. Look, he sent me a check to pay me back."

Tammy hugged Carl. The amount of Tony's check was the exact amount of the check she had put in the offering plate.

Everything belongs to God because everything comes from God. We are mere stewards of His gracious gifts. Acknowledge His loving generosity by sharing what you have, thus honoring His Holy name in the process.

$

Forgive me, Lord, when I want to hoard that which You have amply supplied. May I always give back to You with a gracious heart. Thank You for meeting my every need in love.

Set your mind on things above, not on things on the earth.
COLOSSIANS 3:2 NKJV

Satan uses a vacant mind as a dumping ground.

SPACE FOR RENT

OFTEN WE ALLOW ALL KINDS OF THOUGHTS TO TAKE UP RESIDENCE IN OUR MINDS WITHOUT A SCREENING APPLICATION TO QUALIFY THEM TO RESIDE THERE. Do you sometimes feel you have a Space for Rent sign posted onto your heart or mind?

It's amazing how one negative comment by a complete stranger can move into your mind and quickly fill up every corner; evicting other, more positive thoughts. Or a simple mistake can start a chain reaction of self-criticism that consumes all the space in your mind, closing the blinds and slamming the doors against any reasonable thoughts to the contrary.

God's Word has a lot to say about what kinds of thoughts we should allow to rent space. He knows that giving negative, self-critical thoughts the keys to your mind is a waste of valuable space. We need to be diligent landlords of our thoughts, allowing only the ones God approves. In Philippians 4:8, the Apostle Paul lists the screening criteria we should apply to each thought—We are to allow into our minds only those thoughts that are pure, lovely, admirable, excellent, or praiseworthy.

God is present in our lives to help us screen each thought that tries to come into our minds. If we call on Him to help us refuse entry to thoughts that don't line up with this list of qualifications, we can be sure that there's plenty of space available for those that are pleasing to God. The kind of thoughts we can feel good about welcoming in any time— even when you feel Him standing right next to you.

Do you ever rely on TV, radio, the Web, and print media to provide you with emotional knowledge and opinions? God wants you to turn to Him for direction. He will never lead you astray or confuse the facts.

§

*Lord, too often I take the easy route, allowing other people, the media,
and public opinion to tell me what to think, to believe, and to do.
Forgive me. You're my sole source of wisdom and direction.
May I seek You and Your leading so I will become a woman of biblical
integrity and character.*

The Lord will guide you always;
he will satisfy your needs in a sun-scorched land.
ISAIAH 58:11

A problem not worth prayer is not worth worry.

THE ALTERNATOR BELT

During a weak moment, Kimberly agreed to serve as a chaperone for her daughter's mission trip. However, once the group arrived in Mexico and started their project of building a church in a rural community, Kimberly had to admit she enjoyed it.

One of the jokes among the group was the rattletrap van that transported them to and from their hotel daily. It was incredibly noisy, and its billowing fumes could possibly serve as the worst source of pollution in the entire country.

Three days into the project, the inevitable happened—miles from nowhere, the van broke down. Peering under the hood, the driver announced that the alternator belt had disintegrated. It looked like their only option was to wait for someone to drive by and give one of them a lift back into town.

Suddenly, 16-year-old Nick said, "Hey, let's hold hands around the van and pray!"

Kimberly thought it was a goofy idea to bother God with something she thought so trivial, but they held hands and prayed for the van to be restored. Afterward, a few of the students decided to take a stroll along the side of the road while they waited for help. They hadn't been gone long when they came running back with what appeared to be a brand-new rubber belt. "We were just walking along, and there it was, lying on the road," Jessica chirped. It fit the van perfectly.

Before they continued their trip, Kimberly suggested they again hold hands around the van and thank God for the alternator belt. Nick said, "Wait till they hear about this back home!"

It's easy to dismiss the possibility of divine intervention in today's world. But God is as much at work now as ever. Nothing is too great or too small for His attention. You can count on it.

Thank You, Lord, for being accessible to me when I need You, no matter when or where that may be. Thanks, too, for reminding me that miracles are simply Your way of saying, "I'm here and I'm listening. Call me."

*Blessed is she who has believed that
what the Lord has said to her will be accomplished!*
LUKE 1:45

She who trusts in herself is lost. She who trusts in God can do all
things.

A MIRACLE CALLED
MICHAEL

"I THINK THERE'S A PROBLEM," DR. FRANKLIN TOLD
SARAH. He went on to explain that her most recent ultrasound indi-
cated a critical defect in the development of her baby boy.

This can't be, she thought. *This is the baby my husband and I trusted
God for.*

She agreed to have an amniocentesis, and went home in tears. Brad
cried too when he heard that their precious baby had less than a 50 percent chance of survival through the next five months before his birth.
Even if he did make it, he was certain to have profound brain damage.

When the test results verified the doctor's suspicions, he gently suggested an abortion. Without hesitation, Sarah said, "No—my husband
and I will not be the cause of his death."

As the days passed, the members of Sarah and Brad's church set up
a round-the-clock prayer chain for Baby Michael. And while Dr.
Franklin was amazed that the pregnancy continued without incident,

Sarah and Brad weren't surprised. In fact, by the time the baby was due, they were confident he would be the healthy baby God had promised them.

The day Michael was born, Dr. Franklin stopped by Sarah's hospital room to congratulate her and Brad on their beautiful, healthy baby. He also asked about their church. "I always thought, as a doctor, that I knew everything. Baby Michael has proven to me I don't. I really need God in my life."

Your faith in God's sovereignty and how you invest yourself in it is evident to everyone around you. God will always use you and your total abandonment to His will to reach, teach, and touch others.

§

God, use me and my circumstances however You desire as a way to reveal Yourself to other people. I trust You because I know You honor Your promises. May every generation praise and revere Your name.

If you need wisdom—if you want to know what
God wants you to do—ask him, and he will gladly tell you.
JAMES 1:5 NLT

When you have read the Bible, you will know
it is the Word of God because you will have found in it the key to
your own heart, your own happiness and your own duty.

FACTS ABOUT FAKES

WHEN YOU HEAR THE WORD COUNTERFEIT, THE FIRST THING THAT USUALLY COMES TO MIND IS MONEY. In fact, the practice of counterfeiting money goes back to the earliest days of our country and has been a popular crime ever since. The federal government has gone to great lengths to design currency that's counterfeit-proof, but with each new design there's a new group of counterfeiters who figure out ways to duplicate it.

Counterfeiting is not just limited to money. Sooner or later, those looking to make an easy buck will counterfeit anything of value. Gems are so well counterfeited that it can be difficult for the layperson to tell a real diamond from a fake. There have even been reports of drugs, airplane parts, and even name brand soft drinks "faked" throughout the world.

In the realm of faith, many counterfeit ideas are also passed off as truth. They are counterfeit because they are not based on the Bible. As

Christians, we must be careful to seek God's wisdom about new ideas we encounter. Many are counterfeit, passing themselves off as the truth. Every time we encounter a new idea, we must test it against the filter of God's Word to ensure it is indeed the truth.

And if we're not sure about something, all we need to do is pray for God's wisdom. James 1:5 reminds us that God will guide us. He is always close by, ready to fill our hearts with his reassuring presence, and our minds with His wisdom. He wants us to test everything by what He has revealed through His Word. Only then can we be sure that the truths we hold are ones to bank on.

Just as a carpenter relies on a plumb line to achieve accurate measurements, so we must use God's Word to determine absolute Truth. The more we read and study the Bible, the better able we are to discern fact from fiction.

♪

God, I am grateful for Your Word that leads me in the way of Truth for every situation of my life. I know I will never lose my way as long as I rely on Scripture to direct me home.

"All things you ask in prayer, believing, you shall receive."
MATTHEW 21:22 NASB

You can learn many things from children.
How much patience you have, for instance.

FROM THE MOUTHS OF BABES

GOD, THIS IS NOT THE WAY TO GET RICH TO TURN TO YOU, THOUGHT DIANE. For years, Diane, a Christian, had tried to persuade her husband to accept Jesus as Savior. But now, Rich had been laid off from his job, and she was sure it was only going to prove his point—there's no such thing as a loving God.

Although Rich refused to have anything to do with Christianity, he allowed Diane to go to church. She was a faithful member, and she made sure that her preschool-aged children, Sammy and Bethany, were involved too. Trust me, God responded to her thoughts.

Diane took a sales position at the mall to make ends meet while Rich was between jobs, and he was happy to stay at home with the children. One evening after Sammy and Bethany were asleep, Diane and Rich sat in the den, catching up with the other's day. "Anything happen at home today?" Diane asked.

"Yes," Rich responded. "Believe it or not, I accepted Christ as my Savior."

"What!" Diane shouted.

"Yes," Rich chuckled. "Sammy and Bethany are really good witnesses." He went on to describe how, since he had been staying at home, the children's simple faith began to speak to his heart. As they shared what they learned in Sunday school, talked openly about Jesus' love, and lived their faith with their whole hearts, he realized what his life was missing.

Later, as Diane thanked God for Rich's salvation, she also asked forgiveness for second-guessing His ways.

Like sponges, children soak up everything they hear and see. So, if they learn about the things of God, you can rest assured they will pour out His Spirit to everyone around them. God's witnesses come in all sizes, and their impact penetrates the hardest of hearts.

🎵

Forgive me, God, when I second-guess Your plans. Thank You for working through those I least expect, like children, so Your miraculous power is evident. I shout for joy when a lost soul comes into Your Kingdom.

*Now is your time of grief, but I will see you again
and you will rejoice, and no one will take away your joy.*
JOHN 16:22

She that conceals her grief finds no remedy for it.

SORROW TO JOY

AT 11:30 P.M., DENISE AWOKE FROM A DEEP SLEEP TO THE RINGING PHONE. In the split second before answering, she thought, *something's happened to Jeff.* It was Friday night, and her 17-year-old son had gone out with his youth group to a late movie. The voice on the phone confirmed her fear—there had been an accident. Later, while at the hospital, Denise learned that on his way home, Jeff had died when he was hit head-on by a drunk driver.

The days before Jeff's funeral were a blur. Denise had no idea she could hurt so much. There were moments when she thought her heart would literally burst. Knowing her church friends were fervently praying for her didn't ease her crushing sorrow.

When several of Jeff's friends asked to speak at his funeral, Denise agreed. She had no idea the power their testimonies would have. Each tearfully related the impact Jeff had on their lives. One said Jeff's prayers and friendship helped him quit drugs. Another told how Jeff had been there for him when his parents divorced. Another said Jeff was the strength of the youth group, encouraging them to keep their eyes on God.

As Denise listened to the testimonies, some of her sorrow began to lift. She could almost hear God say, *Jeff is not gone. He will always be in the hearts of those in whose lives he made such a tremendous difference.*

Denise left the church praising God, her heart beginning to feel a glimmer of joy.

Losing a loved one is always painful. Losing a child can seem unbearable. God understands loss. Reach out to Him in times of pain and grief and embrace the comfort of knowing a loved one made a difference to others.

§

Be with me in my time of grief, Lord. And help me to be understanding of those around me who have experienced loss.

Thus the Lord used to speak to Moses
face to face, just as a man speaks to his friend.
EXODUS 33:11 NASB

God doesn't call us to be successful. He calls us to be faithful.

ATTENTION, PLEASE!

THE FIRST YEAR OF OUR LIVES, WE WORKED TO BE ABLE TO STAND ON OUR OWN TWO FEET AND THEN ACTUALLY TAKE A FEW HESITANT STEPS. The glory of this accomplishment faded fast when we realized the world wasn't made for short people. We spent the next three years talking to people's knees, pulling on pant legs and hems to get attention, and begging for a "lift up."

Remember how special you felt when a grown-up actually took the time to get down on your level for a face-to-face conversation? If not, try it with a little one, and watch how their face lights up. Remember those times when an adult lifted you up and carried you on their shoulders. Wow! You could see forever from way up there. Perhaps you imagined you owned the world.

Although we serve the God of the universe, a God so awesome and powerful our minds can't begin to comprehend His majesty, He is always reaching down, communicating with us on our level. He doesn't consider our concerns to be little or childish. He takes them seriously, and we can feel free any time to "tug on God's pant leg" for a face-to-face conversation.

When we need a lift up, He's there to carry us on His shoulders, to give us a look at the world from His perspective. What a tremendous privilege to be able to get the full, loving attention of almighty God any time we ask, day or night!

Have you ever felt like the whole world has turned away? God will never turn away, and He will never leave you alone. He is more than a God to worship; He is God of the universe, and God of your heart. Look up. He's always there.

§

Thank You, Lord for being my best friend. You are always there for me—even when I mess up. Oh, what love!

The Lord said to him, "Who gave man his mouth? . . .
Is it not I, the Lord? Now go; I will help you speak
and will teach you what to say."
EXODUS 4:11-12

**The world is far more ready to receive the
gospel than Christians are to share it.**

THE CELL
PHONE

CLAIRE REFUSED TO BUY A CELL PHONE. In fact, the only thing she disliked more than cell phones was the people who use them. She hated to stand behind someone chattering away in the middle of a grocery store aisle, unconscious of someone else trying to get by. And it baffled her why people thought they could carry on meaningful phone conversations and drive at the same time.

The last straw came when Claire was at the gym. Unbelievably, the woman on the treadmill next to hers pulled a phone out of her sweat pants pocket, dialed a number, and launched into a tense, private conversation.

Claire could tell the woman was talking to her husband who was upset about something she had done. The woman offered excuses, but Claire could tell the man on the other end was becoming angrier. Finally, when the conversation ended, the woman returned the phone to her pocket.

Claire couldn't believe it—she actually felt sorry for the woman. She felt God nudging her to say something.

"Are you okay?" Claire asked. The woman responded with an apology for having bothered her.

"That's all right." Claire couldn't believe the words actually came from her mouth. As they spent the rest of their workout talking about relationship problems, Claire had the opportunity to share about Jesus. Afterward, they agreed to meet the next day for coffee to continue their conversation. On her way home, Claire said aloud, "Okay, God, you showed me. You really can use anything to Your glory—even a cell phone!"

Sometimes God uses the most unlikely people, things, and situations to reveal His glory. Never underestimate how He may use you!

§

Lord, may I be available and willing for You to use me. Even when I may not understand what's going on, I trust You with the results and the methods. May Your Holy Spirit find me acceptable for Your purposes.

Patient endurance is what you need now, so you will continue to do God's will. Then you will receive all that he has promised.
HEBREWS 10:36 NLT

The reward of a thing well done is to have done it.

A HAPPY ENDING

COLLEEN LOVED WRITING. While her children were growing up she hadn't had much time to write, but the day after her youngest child left for college, she sat down at the computer. Soon she had a book of children's stories.

Colleen knew God directed her in writing the stories, and now she felt Him tug at her heart to publish them. But she didn't know the first thing about finding a publisher. When she heard about an upcoming conference for children's writers, she immediately registered. Several publishers' representatives would be there. Perhaps one of them would produce her book. However, at the end of the conference Colleen's enthusiasm turned to discouragement when she learned that only one in 20 thousand submitted manuscripts are ever published.

One evening during a workshop, she slipped outside for some fresh air when she ran into a publisher also playing hooky. They began to talk, and before she knew it, Colleen poured out her fear that her work was no good but that God kept telling her to find a publisher. When the publisher asked to see her manuscript, Colleen hesitated. But he insisted, and Colleen agreed to send him a copy.

More than a month after mailing her manuscript, Colleen received a letter from the publisher. She left it on the table, unable to read the rejection she knew it contained. Finally, her husband, tired of waiting, opened it. He read, "Dear Colleen, God is right. Your book needs to be published, and we're just the company to do it!"

God's timing is perfect. Never doubt it. Be flexible to His leading and anticipate great results. He loves to see the look of amazement on our faces when we allow Him to open the doors of opportunity.

§

God, help me to know when to get out of the way and follow Your leading. Your ways are always better than mine. Thank You for having confidence in me and providing opportunities.

Charm is deceptive, and beauty is fleeting;
but a woman who fears the Lord is to be praised.
PROVERBS 31:30

Though we travel the world over to find the beautiful,
we must carry it with us or we find it not.

A WOMAN
WORTH ENVYING

THEY WERE CALLED "WANNABES"—GIRLS DURING THE
LATE 1980S WHO DRESSED LIKE, ACTED LIKE, AND WANTED
TO BE LIKE POP SINGER MADONNA. From Grace Kelly in the
1950s, the glamorous wife of a prince, to Britney Spears, the perky
blonde with loads of money and an endless supply of energy, there has
never been a shortage of women whose lives we'd gladly trade for our
own!

But it's not just the celebrity women on magazine covers we want to
be like. Sometimes we wish we were the woman in the fancy house
across town, the woman who just had a face lift and now looks ten years
younger, or the one with the perfect children who excel at everything.

No wonder we're shocked when we hear that the perfect life of one
of these women falls apart and she checks into a rehab center for drug
addicts, is served divorce papers by her husband of 30 years, or tries to
end her life.

The truth is—no one's life is perfect. Each woman, no matter what her situation, deals with the temptations and the problems that come along with being human. That's why God wants us to redirect the time we spend envying other women toward making our own lives everything they can be in Him. We need to be aware of God's presence in our lives and His voice saying, *I love you for who you are in Me.* He wants you to become the kind of woman others envy—not for your looks, fame or possessions, but for our love of God and others.

We know beauty is only skin deep, but we often put too much emphasis on outer beauty instead of inner beauty. God knows us inside and out, and He desires for each of us to be known for our beautiful relationship with Him. That's ultimate success.

§

Forgive me, Father, when I am tempted to compare myself to others or to covet their worldly successes. You have blessed me with the best gift of all, Your presence in my life and Your Spirit in my heart. Thank You.

To you, O Lord, I lift up my soul.
Turn to me and have mercy on me, for I am alone and in deep distress.
PSALM 25:1, 16 NLT

Kindness is the insignia of a loving heart.

LUCY'S BIRTHDAY SURPRISE

WALL STREET—IT WAS LUCY'S DREAM COME TRUE. Being from a small Midwest town, she never imagined she could land a job at a world-renowned investment company. On the job for a month, Lucy found living in New York an exciting adventure and her new job to be everything she had hoped.

At the same time, she was desperately lonely. Besides her co-workers, she didn't know a single soul in New York. When she woke up on October 5th—her birthday—she wanted to cry. There was no one to celebrate with, no one to throw her a surprise party, and no one to bake her a cake. At least it was a weekday, and Lucy hoped that work would keep her from sinking into a pity party.

As she left her apartment for the subway, Lucy saw something bright next to her door. It was a single red rose. Curious, she picked it up. Then when she arrived at the office, much to her surprise, she found another red rose on her desk. Just like the rose by her door, there was no note, no indication who had left it. But the surprise wasn't over. When Lucy reached her home that evening, a whole bouquet of red roses stood in a beautiful vase in front of her door. Again, no indication of who the sender might be. She was stunned, but what a wonderful birthday surprise!

Lucy never found out who left her the gift of roses on her birthday. But she would always remember that day as the one when God Himself made her feel loved—just when she needed it most.

Unexplained blessings are the best kind—especially if they pop up when we need them most. It is good to know God loves us so much that He is sensitive to our emotional needs as well as our physical ones.

§

Lord, I do get lonely at times—even when there are other people around. No one knows me like You do. Only You can fill that special place in my heart with Your presence and Your mercy. I am glad You are in my life!

Who is this that appears like the dawn, fair as the moon,
bright as the sun, majestic as the stars in procession?
SONG OF SONGS 6:10

Joy is love exalted.

THE RIDE
OF HER LIFE

LATELY, CATHY BEGAN TO EXPLORE CHRISTIAN MATCH-
MAKING WEB SITES, HOPING TO FIND SOMEONE WHO NOT
ONLY SHARED HER FAITH IN GOD BUT ALSO HER DESIRE TO
RIDE EVERY ROLLER COASTER IN THE COUNTRY! Cathy's fam-
ily already considered her an old maid at age 32. It wasn't that she did-
n't want to get married. She just hadn't found the right guy. In the meantime, she spent her time with the church singles group. She knew God
would bring her the perfect husband—probably when she least expected it.

For weeks, Cathy looked forward to the singles group trip to a local
amusement park with a great roller coaster. But when they arrived at the
park, no one was game for the "Double Twister Sidewinder." So Cathy
went by herself, paired up in a car with a young man who introduced
himself as Dan.

Just as they reached the summit before the first drop, the cars jerked
to a halt. Cathy and Dan looked at each other. "We're stuck!" they said

at the same time. For the next two hours, the cars sat, suspended a hundred feet above the ground.

With nothing else to do, Cathy and Dan talked. The ease of their conversation felt as though they had known each other all along. *He's the one,* she thought and she was sure she heard God whisper a gentle, *Yes,* to her heart. When the cars began to move again, rolling slowly backwards into the loading dock, they couldn't believe how time had flown by. Cathy didn't even mind that she hadn't experienced the thrill of the ride—she had a feeling that she had a ticket for an even more exciting adventure, one named Dan

---

God made you to love others and to be loved. From love, you can experience life's greatest contentment and joy. God knows this about you because He made you in His image. He will not disappoint you.

§

Lord, You bring so many wonderful people into my life, but I believe there is a special place in my heart for the one whom You have selected just for me. I pray for the patience to wait for Your divine intervention and the wisdom to recognize it, knowing You will bring about great joy in the process.

We know that all things work together
for good to those who love God.
ROMANS 8:28 NKJV

The Lord is my strength and my salvation . . . in Him I trust.

TRUSTING THE AUTHOR

MANY WHO ENJOY READING NOVELS KNOW THAT THE
FIRST FEW CHAPTERS ARE LIKELY TO PROVE CONFUSING.
Characters who seem to have nothing to do with each other are introduced. Disconnected events take place, and subplots come from different directions. But you continue to read because you know that at some
point, the author will bring the characters, events, and subplots together to ultimately make sense.

In many ways, life is the same. Things often happen to us that seem
to make no sense.

Why are my teens so defiant? Why did the business we worked so
hard to build go bankrupt? Why did our best friend suddenly quit calling?

To our confusion, God responds, *Keep reading!* No matter what happens, He wants us to trust that He will bring everything together in the
end. In Scripture are many examples of people who were confused about
the events in their lives. Mary questioned how God could use her to bear

His Son ("How will this be... since I am a virgin?" Luke 1:34). Jesus even asked God to change the plan for His life ("My Father, if it is possible, may this cup be taken from me." Matthew 26:39).

But God said, "Keep reading." Ultimately, Mary and Jesus trusted God, the divine Author, to work through them and the events of their lives to His ultimate glory. He wants us to do the same.

We often want to read the story's ending before completing the book. But in life, God doesn't allow us to know the ending before experiencing the parts that make the end worthwhile. Live each day to its fullest and to God's glory!

§

God, You know I am impatient at times and want to do it all now. But Your Word reminds me that You have a plan for me, and that You have orchestrated every detail. May I learn to live each day as it comes, knowing the end of this story promises to be better than its beginning.

As each one has received a special gift,
employ it in serving one another, as good stewards
of the manifold grace of God.
1 PETER 4:10 NASB

Often the greatest talents lie unseen.

THROUGH
GOD'S EYES

WENDY FELT CONVICTED. It seemed every time she opened her Bible, God led her to verses about finding the best in others. Just this morning in the Sunday service, her pastor preached a powerful sermon about how Jesus noticed and cared for those whom the rest of the world overlooked. Wendy prayed, *God, make me sensitive to others. Help me to see everyone the way You see them.*

Later that week, Wendy met the ladies in their book club for a pizza and video party. Afterward, it looked like a tornado had hit the fellowship hall. Wendy made a pass with a trash bag, but she was tired, and besides, Ethel would finish up. Ethel was the woman who had faithfully cleaned the church for the past 20 years. It seemed no one thought about her unless there was a mess to clean up.

Wendy was almost home when she realized she had forgotten her Bible. Bummed out, she drove back. Upon entering the fellowship hall, she was amazed to hear beautiful piano music. She peeked around the corner to see who was playing—it was Ethel. Wendy waited until Ethel finished the elegant Chopin Etude before making her presence known with enthusiastic applause. Embarrassed, Ethel apologized and went back to cleaning up the mess.

As Wendy drove home, she thanked God for answering her prayer in such a creative way. She felt him say, Now you see Ethel like I do—a unique person with something beautiful to give. Wendy would never take Ethel, or anyone else, for granted again.

Isn't it terrific to see God expressed through the gifts and talents of others? Everyone is precious in His sight. May we learn to see them as precious in our eyes too.

♪

Lord, You are the One who fashioned the universe and
set the tides in motion. You also gave each of us special gifts and talents
that are uniquely our own. May we express them with passion
and learn to appreciate others in a way that is pleasing
and acceptable to You.

Be even-tempered, content with second place,
quick to forgive an offense. Forgive as quickly
and completely as the Master forgave you.
COLOSSIANS 3:13 MSG

Forgiveness of sins. This alone is the Gospel,
and this is the life and immortality brought to life by Jesus.

ALL IN THE FAMILY

DARLENE DREADED THE FAMILY GATHERING, BUT THERE WAS NO WAY TO GET AROUND IT. Her mother was dying, and the doctors said that it was time to gather the family. The problem—everyone in her family hated each other. Her five brothers and sisters, along with their spouses, had feuded for as long as she could remember.

When her siblings crowded into Darlene's living room, there was an icy silence. Darlene hoped that coffee and her famous strawberry shortcake would break the ice, but it didn't. Finally, she took a deep breath and said a quick, silent prayer. *God, help me say something that will bring my family back together.* Surprisingly, what came out was a story, a memory about the time her mother stayed up all night reading *Winnie the Pooh* to her when she had the chicken pox. When she finished, her brother Chuck shared a memory of the time their mother sat through the pouring rain to cheer on his junior high football team. One after another, each of Darlene's brothers, sisters, and their husbands and wives shared memories of their mother. Before long, they were laughing together at the funny memories, wiping away tears at the poignant ones.

When the afternoon was turning into evening, the conversation changed. The group began apologizing to each other with hugs and tears for the years of bad feelings and lost time together. Darlene was overwhelmed by the way God had worked—He had used her and a memory about her mother to open the floodgates of forgiveness. She ended their evening with a prayer, thanking God for her mother's life and for bringing her family back together in such an unexpected and beautiful way.

Funny how seeds of unforgiveness and jealousy can grow into towering forests of separation, even among the people we know the best. Learn to forgive first; it can prepare the way for great healing.

§

Even when I don't want to forgive another person, Lord, convict me of my pride and urge me to forgive anyway. Forgiveness is better than a balm is to a wound. It restores and replenishes tenfold, making my life pleasing to You.

"There is nothing to fear. From now on you'll be fishing for men and women." They pulled their boats up on the beach, left them, nets and all, and followed him.
LUKE 5:10-11 MSG

What would life be if we had no courage to attempt anything?

MAKING AN IMPRESSION

THE DREAM OF EVERY SKIER IS TO BE THE FIRST ON A SLOPE AFTER A FRESH SNOWFALL, MAKING THE FIRST SET OF TRACKS ON A SMOOTH SURFACE. Likewise, speedboat drivers enjoy leaving their mark, a wake fanning out behind them, on a smooth surface of water. And who hasn't seen evidence of where a jet has been from the white vapor trail left behind?

As Christian women, we should also work to leave evidence of where we've been. Do you strive to make an impression for God's Kingdom in the lives of your family, co-workers, fellow church members, and friends?

Doing what God prompts us to do often makes waves. That is not easy with today's pressure to conform, to go with the flow and, under no circumstances, upset the status quo. When we risk making an impression in Christ's name, we sometimes also risk our jobs, our social status, and others' acceptance.

her tears, Margaret noticed something lying in the ashes next to the steps. She bent down and picked up their wedding album.

Margaret and Jim were baffled at the strange appearance of the album. It wasn't even singed. As they leafed through the album's pages, recalling the happiest day of their life, they both knew God had saved this album for them, to remind them that even though their house was gone, they still had each other and Him. What else did they really need?

Though loss of any kind is painful, it's important to realize that the things of earth are fleeting. But our relationship with the Lord is infinite, and He promises to restore our broken hearts if we willingly give everything back to Him.

§

Lord, help me to let go and let You have control over every aspect of my life. When things happen beyond my control, may I choose to find gratitude in Your protection as I acknowledge Your goodness toward me.

He will give beauty for ashes, joy instead of mourning,
praise instead of despair. For the Lord has planted
them like strong and graceful oaks for his own glory.
ISAIAH 61:3 NLT

God's fingers can touch nothing but to mould it into loveliness.

UNEXPECTED BEAUTY

AMY WAS DEVASTATED WHEN SHE LEARNED THE DIAG-NOSIS. The doctors rushed her through surgery to remove the lump, and now she faced six months of chemotherapy. She prayed desperately that God would make something beautiful out of the pain and ugliness left from cancer.

Every three weeks Amy went for treatment. She watched while toxins designed to kill cancer cells dripped into her arm. She didn't know about killing cancer cells, but the medication certainly did a good job of making her hair fall out. Still she prayed, *God, I know you can make something beautiful out of anything—even this.*

Week after week dragged by. Much of the time, Amy felt too ill to do anything but lie on the couch and watch old movies. Still she prayed.

Suddenly, while the nurse was hooking her up to the IV for a treatment, Amy realized the beauty she prayed for was in the people's faces who had cared for her. Everyone, from this nurse to the cancer center receptionist to the oncologist—all were the kindest people she had ever met. They had gone out of their way to answer her questions, listen to her fears, and speak words of hope. They had been examples of compassion that Amy herself hoped to be to others.

As she sat there, being ministered to by this caring nurse, she thanked God for His picture of real beauty in the kind hands, hopeful words, ready smiles, and genuine concern of others.

We can find God's beauty in the splendor of the mountain meadow as well as the subtle kindness of a stranger. Its form is not important, but we must recognize its source and always offer praises of gratitude.

§

Lord, You are beautiful to me, especially in the details of my everyday world. When trials and challenges come, I want to see something beautiful in them. Give me eyes to see beauty in everything.

What? know ye not that your body is the temple of the Holy Ghost which is in you, which ye have of God, and ye are not your own?
1 CORINTHIANS 6:19 KJV

Every flower of the field, every fiber of a plant,
every particle of an insect, carries with it the imprint of its Maker.

PRESERVING THE HOLY SPIRIT'S HABITAT

THE PASSENGER PIGEON, LABRADOR DUCK, STELLER'S SEA COW, AND QUAGGA ZEBRA—THESE ARE AMONG THE MORE THAN 50 SPECIES OF BIRDS AND 75 SPECIES OF MAMMALS THAT HAVE BECOME EXTINCT DURING THE LAST 200 YEARS. The extinction of the world's animal and plant life is a serious concern, one that both government and private organizations have spent millions of dollars trying to prevent.

The primary reason that species become extinct is the loss of their habitat or, simply, the place where they live. For example, 86,400 acres of the world's rain forests are destroyed every day to make way for farming, mining, or other ventures. For the thousands of species of animals and plants that live in these forests, the destruction of their habitat typically means the loss of their lives. Another reason for species endangerment is pollution from sources like pesticides, energy processing, and automobile emissions.

For animals and plants to survive, they must be nurtured in a healthy environment where they receive all they need to grow and thrive.

Likewise, we must make sure our hearts are a healthy place where God's Holy Spirit can live. If we destroy the Holy Spirit's "habitat" by crowding it with other priorities or polluting it with unconfessed sin, we will endanger the Holy Spirit's power in our lives. We must be vigilant about making our hearts a pure and nurturing environment for God's Spirit to grow and thrive so that we can continually enjoy His presence in our lives.

Just as the beasts of the field and the birds of the air require a healthy place to dwell and flourish, so does God's Holy Spirit. Let's strive to keep our hearts and minds pure of negative and dishonoring thoughts and desires so He will be evident in all we do.

§

My soul belongs to You, O Lord. May I always seek to protect it from the misery and temptation of wickedness. I desire for my heart and soul to be a healthy place for You to dwell always.

He took the children in his arms,
put his hands on them and blessed them.
MARK 10:16

**No one ever really finds out what she
believes in until she begins to instruct her children.**

MOM'S LITTLE HELPER

MELISSA HAD METICULOUSLY PLANNED TONIGHT'S SUR-
PRISE BIRTHDAY PARTY FOR HER HUSBAND, TOM. She had
given explicit instructions to the party guests about what time to show
up and where to park their cars so he wouldn't suspect anything when
he arrived home from the office.

Melissa's four-year-old daughter, Rachel, was as excited about the
birthday party as Melissa. Now with the decorations up and gifts
wrapped, the two worked on the last job before the party—the cake. It
was going to be a triple-layer double fudge cake with icing an inch thick.
Rachel sat on a stool by the kitchen counter, watching her mother sift
flour, crack eggs, and stir melted chocolate into a big mixing bowl.
Melissa had just finished the batter when the phone rang.

When Melissa returned to the kitchen, she was horrified to find that
Rachel had dumped the rest of the carton of eggs, shells and all, into the
bowl and was smashing them into the batter with her hands. "Look,

Mommy! I'm helping you make Daddy's cake!"

Melissa felt the heat of anger rise. "Rachel! You've ruined it!" Rachel instantly dissolved into tears and begged her mother's forgiveness through hiccupped sobs. But Melissa felt God's hand on her shoulder as He whispered into her heart, *You should ask Rachel for forgiveness. What if I blew up every time you made a mistake?*

Melissa's anger was quickly replaced with shame as she realized that she had wounded her daughter's sweet, giving heart. After apologizing and asking Rachel to forgive her, Melissa hugged her daughter and asked for her help to make another cake.

How precious is the life and company of children! Yes, they're sticky at times and irritable at others. But they remind us how much God loves us, and how He gives us the opportunity to impact others in significant and loving ways.

$

My greatest challenge and my greatest desire, Lord, is to be the kind of parent, relative, or friend worthy of the beautiful children You've brought into my life. Help me to listen, instruct, and guide each one with sensitivity, compassion, and mercy.

*Children shouldn't have to look out
for their parents; parents look out for the children.*
2 CORINTHIANS 12:14 MSG

The most valuable gift you can give another is a good example.

A TOUGH CHOICE

THE ENVY OF EVERY OTHER WOMAN AT AMCOR, VICTORIA AWOKE TO A CRYING THREE-YEAR-OLD. This was the day she was to receive the Employee of the Year award. Over the years, Victoria had worked hard to advance at Amcor. Now, as director of the accounting division, she was reaping the rewards of her diligence.

Victoria checked the temperature of her three-year-old while she urged her other two children to "snap it up, we're going to be late." Thank goodness Ellen's temperature was only slightly elevated, still within daycare center limits.

As soon as she reached the office, however, the phone rang. It was the center. Ellen's temperature was dangerously high, and she had been taken to the emergency room. As Victoria drove to the hospital, a voice inside her kept saying, *It's time to leave Amcor.*

Sure enough, Victoria missed the awards ceremony, but for some reason it didn't matter. After talking it over with her husband, she made an appointment to see her boss. When she walked into his office, he began to shower her with compliments for her outstanding performance. She stopped him and said, "It's been a privilege for me to work for this great company. But today, I'm giving my notice. It may sound strange, but after all these years of God's hand on my work here, now He's leading me in a completely different direction."

But Victoria began to doubt her decision as she packed her office. Then suddenly His presence filled the room and He reassured her, *Amcor will be fine without you. And if you trust Me, you're going to be fine too!.*

It's easy for celebrity to hold our attention. Our human nature seems to feed on it. But as mature Christians, we must decipher attention from responsibility. Our greatest recognition comes from filling the roles God provides us as spouse, parent, and friend. First things first.

§

God, You know I often struggle with the desire for others to recognize and reward my contributions. And though that's not bad in and of itself, I cannot allow this desire to distort my view of what is really important in life. Please help me see my family priorities clearly, knowing they offer me the greatest satisfaction and the ultimate reward for a job well done.

He Himself has said, "I will never desert you,
nor will I ever forsake you."
HEBREWS 13:5 NASB

Have a vision not clouded by fear.

WINNERS IN CHRIST

ONE OF THE MOST SUSPENSE-FILLED EVENTS AT THE SUMMER OLYMPICS IS THE BALANCE BEAM. It's amazing to watch muscled gymnasts perform complicated acrobatic moves on a 4" wide surface. Concentration is just as important as physical strength. One tiny miscalculation or break in concentration, and the gymnast's balance fails. It doesn't matter which side of the beam the gymnast falls off. Right or left, they've lost the competition.

Sometimes being Christian is like living on a balance beam. We may feel pressured to make all the right decisions, make all the right moves, perform perfectly, and never relax, or else we risk falling off and losing the competition. But God doesn't want us to live life on a balance beam. He knows that no matter how hard we try, we can never perform perfectly in life. That's why He came to earth, took our place on the cross, and won the competition for us! And not only that, but He is the source of all the strength needed to perform well in life's other events—the motherhood relay, the employment hurdles, and the Sunday School teacher pole vault.

So we can relax. When the going gets tough, we can turn it all over to Jesus, confident that He will be right there to show us the right moves, to help us stay focused, and constantly amaze us by what He can do through us. With Jesus in our lives, we can't possibly lose!

God is with you even when you cannot see, hear, or sense His presence. He holds you upright when life throws you off balance. Stay connected to His leading through daily prayer, and keep your eyes focused on Him!

Father, sometimes I get ahead of myself, thinking I've got everything under control and I don't need to bother You with the details. Forgive my arrogance. Without You I cannot accomplish anything. Help me to remain faithful to Your purpose for me, keeping my attention focused and true.

Have mercy on me, O God, have mercy!
I look to you for protection. I will hide beneath
the shadow of your wings until this violent storm is past.
PSALM 57:1 NLT

God be prais'd, that to believing souls
gives light in darkness, comfort in despair.

IN THE SHADOW
OF HIS WINGS

"HONEY!" CAROL'S EYES POPPED OPEN. Her husband Mitch's call sounded as close as the next room. She looked at the clock—2:34 A.M. Mitch, a major in the Army, had recently been deployed to the Middle East. Fortunately, Carol's parents lived nearby, and members of her church frequently called or stopped by to make sure she was okay.

She drifted off again, a sleepy prayer on her lips.

"Honey!" Carol was jolted awake again. This time she was convinced her husband was calling her. She got up, went downstairs and pulled her Bible from the shelf. Settling into Mitch's easy chair, she read Psalm 57 aloud—"Have mercy on me, O God, have mercy on me, for in you my soul takes refuge. I will take refuge in the shadow of your wings until the disaster has passed." As she read, she envisioned large, white wings surrounding her husband on the battlefield. At the same time, a wave of God's gentle peace washed over her. She continued to pray and read until it was light.

Later, when Mitch returned, he related the horrific events of that day when Carol so clearly heard his voice. His convoy had been ambushed by the enemy, and in the ensuing battle, which lasted three long hours, three of his men were seriously injured. When Carol asked if he was afraid, he said, "No. You know, Honey, I just had a feeling that something, almost like a protective shield, surrounded me." Carol blinked back tears as she hugged her husband tight.

We cannot always be everywhere we think we need to be, but God can and is. Turn to Him for the protection you seek.

§

I realize that as much as I love my family and loved ones, Lord, that You love them even more. Help me to turn to You when I am fearful for their protection, finding solace in Your Word. Thank You for answered prayer.

In God I have put my trust; I shall not be afraid.
PSALM 56:4 NASB

God is faithful, and if we serve him faithfully,
He will provide for our needs.

FINDING THE RIGHT WAY

A WEEKEND AWAY—ALL BY HERSELF. It was the best birthday gift Lisa could imagine. Her husband, understanding her stress as a working mom, paid for her to spend three carefree days at a mountain resort.

After unpacking, Lisa put on her boots and struck out into the woods for a hike. As she walked, her heart overflowed with praise—for her family, for the beauty of nature, for all the wonderful things in her life.

At dusk, Lisa decided to make her way back. But when she looked around, she couldn't find the trail. Swallowing hard, she walked in the direction she felt led to the resort. But it was growing darker, and she still didn't see anything familiar.

On the verge of panic, Lisa spotted a cabin in the distance, a plume of smoke rose from the chimney. She ran to the cabin and banged on the door. When an old man answered, she blurted, "Help me! I'm lost!" He gave her directions back to the resort. Although she followed them precisely, the woods became thicker and darker. She began to doubt the directions, but a voice inside her heart repeatedly said, *Keep going. Trust the directions.*

Nervously, Lisa kept going, and just as night fell, the friendly lights of the resort peeped through the trees to greet her. Taking off her hiking boots in her room, Lisa was glad she had listened to the old man, and to God's voice, both helping her find the way.

When the way appears dark and foreboding, rely on God to see You through. He may use people whom you'd least expect, but you can trust His direction.

Thank You, God, for leading me through the dark shadows of life. Thank You for never leaving me alone. Thank You for providing others to help me through the tough situations.

When some of the teachers of religious law
who were Pharisees saw him [Jesus]
eating with people like that [tax collectors and many other
notorious sinners], they said to his disciples,
"Why does he eat with such scum?"
MARK 2:16 NLT

Jesus is a friend who walks in when the world walks out.

CAR
TALK

THERE ARE TWO PARTS TO MOST CAR DEALERSHIPS. One is the showroom where you find the brand-new cars, polished to a mirror-like shine, bright lights turned toward them to show them off. With well-dressed salespeople eager to show you all the fancy extras of the featured cars, the showroom is meant to impress. Here, image is everything.

The other side of the dealership is the repair shop. The opposite of the showroom, you find dirty, used car parts lying around and cars on racks with uniformed mechanics peering underneath, trying to figure out what's making that grinding noise or front-end shimmy. Here, image doesn't matter.

God wants us as Christian women to be like car repair shops, the kind of people with whom others feel comfortable sharing what's broken in their lives. We should be known as people to whom image doesn't matter, who will welcome any kind of "make" or "model" into our lives.

It's easy to love others who, like new cars, look good, are worth a lot of money, and enhance our social status. The world doesn't want to be associated with those who it sees as "junkers" that look terrible and can barely run. But these are the very people whom Christ views as necessary to the Kingdom of God and close to His heart. Jesus came to save the broken. His presence in our lives fills us with that same compassion and love for others, whether they come to the "showroom floor" or the "repair shop."

Bright lights, shiny features, and good looks naturally attract our attention, but few of us live in such a world. God doesn't want us to idolize the glitz. He wants us to see everyone as significant, regardless of status or origin. Love does not discriminate.

§

Lord, help me to see every person and every circumstance through Your eyes of love. Protect me from focusing on the veneer. Forgive me when I do, and teach me Your ways of seeing value in everyone.

"Those who honor me I will honor,
but those who despise me will be disdained."
1 SAMUEL 2:30

Dignity does not consist in possessing honors,
but in deserving them.

TRUE
FAME

FOR THE THIRD YEAR IN A ROW, KAREN WAS VOTED THE
BEST BROADCAST NEWS ANCHOR IN THE TRI-CITIES AREA.
A KWTV employee for 15 years, she had worked her way up from lowly
reporter with all the worst assignments to number-one anchor. She
couldn't go anywhere without someone stopping her for an autograph or
saying, "Hey, aren't you . . . ?"

Karen tried not to let fame go to her head, but it was difficult. All
her broadcasting colleagues lived for recognition, and they didn't hesitate
to undermine each other if they thought it would put them ahead. Even
Karen had been the victim of vicious back-stabbing by some she had
thought were friends. Every day, she prayed the Lord would help her
remain humble.

Karen kept life in perspective by volunteering in the children's ward
at the local hospital. The atmosphere of children who had suffered some
of life's harshest blows helped her to see things more clearly through

God's eyes. Their courage and hope constantly inspired her. Karen felt others should ask for their autographs.

However, Karen feared her notoriety had penetrated into the children's ward when one afternoon she walked through the door and a new little patient said, "Hey, you're famous!"

"Well, not really!" Karen responded.

"Yes, you are," the little girl insisted. "Everyone told me you're the best checkers player ever. Wanna play with me?"

"Sure thing," Karen said, pulling up a chair and thinking, *Thank you, God, for once again reminding me what's important in Your Kingdom!*

You may never know who is watching you or sizing you up for future reference. But if you live your life in an honorable way, you will not have to worry about the final assessment. And God is watching even when no one else is.

§

Lord, I want to live a life that is pleasing to You.
Whether I make honest mistakes or improve my social status,
I always want to live in such a way that others will see You living in me. That's the best recognition possible!

You are my hiding place; You preserve me from trouble.
PSALM 32:7 NASB

Beneath God's watchful eye His saints securely dwell;
the hand that bears all nature up shall guard His children well.

OUT OF HARM'S WAY

AT 60 YEARS OLD, LOUISE'S HUSBAND DENNIS DIED SUDDENLY. Although her husband was a Christian and Louise was confident he was now with God in heaven, her grief seemed overwhelming. Her children were relieved when ten months later, Louise began to see friends again and resumed her church activities. They knew for sure she was all right when she called a contractor to add a sitting room onto the house. She had always wanted a bright, sun-filled place to read and do needlepoint, but Dennis said they couldn't afford such an expensive project.

When the room was framed and sheet-rocked, Louise had a party. She couldn't wait for its completion to share her excitement. After her guests left Louise was loading the dishwasher when she heard a voice call her. At first she thought she had only imagined it, but then she heard it again. It sounded anxious, insistent. She followed the voice as it continued to call her, leading her to the new addition. There she found a pile of insulation partially lying on the space heater she had moved into the room for the party. The insulation was smoldering, on the verge of flames.

Quickly, Louise unplugged the heater, carried the insulation outside, and doused it with water. Her heart was still pounding when she went back inside, but she was filled with gratitude to God for watching over her, for warning her of danger, and for saving her sitting room. Then she chuckled and thought, *See, Dennis, even God wants me to have this room!*

It's comforting to know that our departed loved ones who were Christians are now in heaven. That knowledge encourages us to go on with confidence, thanking God that we will see them again.

§

Lord, thank You for the beautiful people You've brought into my life, both those who are alive and those who've gone on to live with You in glory. Thank You for watching out for and protecting me from harm.

He will wipe every tear from their eyes.
REVELATION 21:4

Christians should judge only to determine how to render aid.

NOT JUST ANOTHER DAY

EVERY DAY WAS THE SAME ROUTINE. Erin was at the bus stop precisely at 7:09 A.M. to catch the 7:10 bus. During the forty-minute ride into downtown, she always read the newspaper. Then one morning, something inside told her to take a look—a real look—at the people around her. Immediately, she noticed a young woman on the bus who seemed to be profoundly sad.

Amazingly, when she got off the bus, the woman walked to the same office building and walked onto the same elevator as Erin. *Why haven't I noticed her before?* Erin thought when the woman got off on the 12th floor.

At 8 P.M. that evening, Erin, having worked late, rushed to catch the last bus out of downtown. She was annoyed when the elevator stopped at the 12th floor, until the doors opened and the sad young woman entered. The doors had barely closed when Erin felt God prompt her to say, "I saw you on the bus this morning and, well, are you okay?"

The woman's eyes filled with tears. She looked down and softly answered, "No."

The two talked all the way home, then three hours more. The young woman, named Anne, confessed she had been depressed for weeks and was considering suicide to end the pain. Erin persuaded Anne to seek help instead and offered to help her find a good counselor. At midnight, they hugged goodbye, promising to see each other tomorrow morning on the 7:10 bus. And for the first time, Erin saw Anne smile.

With God we realize there are no chance meetings. He directs our paths and weaves our lives together in a beautiful mosaic of ministry as we reach out to one another in love and compassion.

§

Lord, forgive me when I become overly consumed with my routine and my agenda, failing to see those around me who are crying out in pain. Please prevent me from becoming so occupied that I don't see how You want me to serve as a minister of Your love.

Love your neighbor as yourself.
MATTHEW 22:39 NLT

Things do not change; we change.

MEETING NEEDS IN YOUR OWN BACKYARD

ELIZABETH WAS NOT WHAT YOU'D CALL INSENSITIVE TO OTHERS. She volunteered every Wednesday at her church's downtown soup kitchen, she sponsored a child in Ethiopia through a Christian organization, and she gave generously to the annual foreign missions fund-raiser drive. Last year, she had even gone on a mission trip to build a church in a poor community in Honduras. Elizabeth felt confident she was doing a good job to meet others' needs.

That is, until God used an appointment at the hair salon to convince her otherwise. While the stylist washed her hair, Elizabeth overheard two other salon clients talking about a woman whose husband recently walked out on her and her two children. Although he planned to give her the house, her part-time job was barely enough to cover the mortgage. The water drowned out some of their words. In her heart, Elizabeth heard God say, "Pay attention." She listened more carefully. They went on to say they heard the woman didn't have enough money to buy groceries.

Then she heard the woman's name, Elizabeth sat up with a shot, dripping water and shampoo. "What?" she said. "Did you say her name is Dawn? Did you say she lives on Madison Street?" She was shocked to realize the woman they were talking about lived in her neighborhood.

Elizabeth could hardly sit still for the rest of her appointment. Afterwards, she rushed to the grocery store. Then she went immediately to Dawn's house. When Dawn invited her in, Elizabeth offered, along with the bags of food, her apologies for her insensitivity.

Later that night, Elizabeth also apologized to God for overlooking the mission field right in her own neighborhood!

Though God calls some to mission fields in foreign lands, He calls all of us to love the lost, the hurting, the hungry, and the lonely right in our midst. As followers of Jesus Christ, we are on a life-long mission trip—even if we never travel more than a few steps out our back door.

§

Father God, help me to never fail to see individual trees in the forest. Whether You call me to distant lands or not, help me to be prepared day in and day out to share the assurance of my salvation in Christ with everyone.

"You're blessed when you get your inside world—
your mind and heart—put right. Then you can
see God in the outside world."
MATTHEW 5:8 MSG

God answers in the depths, never in the shallows, of our soul.

MOTIVE IS
EVERYTHING

THERE ARE LOTS OF DO'S AND DON'TS IN THE BIBLE. Ever since God told Adam and Eve not to eat the fruit of a certain tree in the Garden of Eden, He has provided His children with rules to follow. In fact, God's rules cover every situation in life from how to conduct business to how to treat our parents. And He has given us His Holy Spirit, who always has His hand on our shoulder, encouraging us to follow God's direction.

However, as we seek to obey God's rules and directions, He wants us to do so out of love and devotion to Him. Unfortunately, we often obey God for selfish reasons, like a child who cleans his room not because he loves and wants to please his parents, but because he knows afterward they will let him play video games.

Think about it. Do we read a passage of Scripture so we can learn how to follow God more closely or so we can check it off our "Read Through the Bible in a Year" plan? Do we invite Christian friends over for dinner so we can get to know them better or so we can show off our gourmet cooking? Do we volunteer for church committees because we feel God calling us to do so or because we want others to consider us leaders?

In other words, when we do anything for God, we should ask ourselves this simple question: Is it about me or is it about God? It's only when we're obeying God from pure motives that it brings honor to Him and His blessing to us.

Though we don't think to do it often, it's important to run a "double-check" on our motives from time to time—especially when we agree to help or serve others. If our response reveals how doing so will benefit ourselves, then we're better off passing and asking God for another opportunity after we've dealt with some core issues in our spiritual life.

§

Father, forgive me when I seek recognition instead of seeking to serve others. This self-serving attitude pops up in some pretty strange places, so help me become aware of those times when I am focused more on myself than on truly serving You.

The angel of the Lord encamps around those
who fear him, and he delivers them.
PSALM 34:7

Angels take different forms at the bidding of their master, God, and thus reveal themselves to people and unveil divine mysteries to them.

THE GUARDIAN ANGEL-DOG

"THAT'S THE ONE," CASSIE SAID. Her husband, John, stared in disbelief. "That runt? That's the ugliest dog in the whole place!"

"I know," Cassie responded. "But I just have a strong feeling he's the one we're supposed to get." John sighed, chalking it up to his wife's hormones still being wacky after the baby's birth.

They named the puppy Buster, and although he was certifiably homely, he was smart. He was house trained within a week, and he would sit for hours, just watching the baby. Cassie joked that he was a guardian angel-dog.

In the evenings, when the baby was finally asleep, Cassie, John, and Buster would pile onto the couch and watch TV. But this particular evening, Buster was restless. He trotted upstairs, then back down, and barked. After he did that several times, Cassie decided he must need to go outside, but when she opened the back door, he sat there, barking.

Finally, Buster disappeared up the stairs again, and the next thing

Cassie and John heard was his shrill bark—coming through the monitor in the baby's room. The couple ran upstairs where they found the reason Buster had been frantically trying to get their attention—the baby had stopped breathing.

Springing into action, Cassie called 911 while John performed CPR. The baby soon began to cry and the color came back into his face—everything was going to be okay. Cassie and John both felt God's presence fill the room at that moment. He felt very near to them, the baby, and Buster.

Cassie patted Buster and said, "God knew you were the right puppy for us. You really are a guardian angel-dog!" Buster just licked her hand.

Only a creative God would think about using unique aspects of His creation to demonstrate His incredible love for us. Never underestimate the powerful and creative nature of the living Lord to protect you and to save you from harm.

§

God, I am grateful for every living thing You have placed on earth and how You use them to warm us, feed us, protect us, warn us, shelter us, and comfort us. Thank You for Your wonderful blessings and for all Your creatures, great and small.

*Everyone present was filled with the Holy Spirit
and began speaking in other languages,
as the Holy Spirit gave them this ability.*
ACTS 2:4 NLT

**The Spirit of God first imparts love;
next inspires hope and then gives liberty.**

SPANISH 101

MOVING TO SAN ANTONIO WAS A CULTURE SHOCK FOR LAURA, WHO HAD GROWN UP IN MAINE. But they couldn't pass up her husband's job opportunity in Texas. To get out of the house and feel useful while she adjusted to her new home, Laura volunteered at a local women's shelter.

The shelter served Hispanic women, many of whom had recently immigrated from Mexico. Laura felt a kinship with these women so far away from everything familiar to them, and she wanted to offer encouragement to them. The problem was—she didn't speak Spanish. She had taken Spanish classes in college, but she didn't remember much.

Laura's inability to speak Spanish relegated her to jobs at the shelter like cooking meals and washing linens. She knew they were important jobs, but she really wanted to be able to talk to the women who so desperately needed to hear loving and compassionate words.

One afternoon while Laura cleaned up after lunch, she saw one of the women, sitting at the table after everyone else had left, quietly crying. Laura's heart broke to see her pain. She pulled up a chair next to the woman. *At least I can hold her hand so she knows someone cares.*

Then without thinking, Laura opened her mouth and started to pray. Through tears, she asked God to protect this precious soul and to fill her heart with His love. It was only when she finished praying and the woman hugged her that Laura realized she had prayed entirely in Spanish.

When we express genuine compassion for others, it is God's way of using us to comfort another. And though several barriers naturally exist among people of different ethnic and cultural backgrounds, the sincerity of love is able to bridge all obstacles.

§

Thank You, Holy Spirit, for interceding on my behalf to the Lord of Hosts. Thank You for giving me the right words and the right attitude of ministry when needed. May You be praised forever!

*We speak as messengers who have been
approved by God to be entrusted with the Good News. Our purpose
is to please God, not people. He is the one who examines the
motives of our hearts.*
1 THESSALONIANS 2:4 NLT

The Church has nothing to do but save souls;
therefore, spend and be spent in this work. It is not necessary to
speak so many times, but to reach souls as you can; bringing as
many sinners as possible to repentance.

BIGGER IS NOT ALWAYS BETTER

IT'S THE AGE OF THE SUPER STORES THAT TAKE UP FOOTBALL FIELD-SIZED SPACES TO SELL EVERYTHING FROM RADISHES TO CAR PARTS. The most well-known mass merchandiser, with annual revenues of a quarter billion dollars, is number-one on the list of Fortune 500 companies. This huge company employs 1.2 million employees around the world and shows no signs of slowing down.

Of course, super stores have their place. But just as important in our lives are our favorite small, independently owned stores. Perhaps you have a neighborhood bookstore where the employees know your name—and reading tastes. Or you wouldn't think of buying a birthday cake anywhere but that quaint little bakery, although there's no convenient parking nearby. Perhaps your favorite dress shop is owned by a woman who calls you periodically about a new, one-of-a-kind outfit that "is just perfect for you, Honey!"

Likewise, in the effort to spread the gospel, massive evangelism crusades have their place. But more often, God taps you on the shoulder and points out someone in whose life He is working and has you work in an intimate, one-on-one relationship. It's when you take the time, like your favorite independent shop owners, to really get to know someone and make their life an important part of your own that God opens hearts. When you really care, others listen as you share the secret to eternal life. Ask God to make you sensitive to others, to make you aware of opportunities to share His love and grace. With His hand on your shoulder you will see with His eyes and work with Him at the tasks He has for you to do.

Unlike some aspects of life where bigger, faster, and newer are the measures of efficiency and effectiveness, we can best reach someone with the gospel of Christ through one-on-one relationships. Some things never need to be improved!

§

Just as Jesus offered forgiveness, addressed individual needs, and healed people one at a time, may I always be ready to spend the time necessary to invest in individuals. Lord, help me to always see the significance of every person, just as you do, and, therefore, listen and love them with an undivided, single-minded heart.

"Do you have any idea how difficult
it is for the rich to enter God's kingdom? Let me tell you,
it's easier to gallop a camel through a needle's eye
than for the rich to enter God's kingdom."
MATTHEW 19:23-24 MSG

Surplus wealth is a sacred trust which its possessor
is bound to administer for the good of the community.

TERRI'S PRIORITY CHECK

TERRI LOOKED AROUND AT HER NEW HOUSE IN THE CITY'S MOST PRESTIGIOUS NEIGHBORHOOD AND BREATHED A PRAYER OF THANKS. She and her husband had worked for years to afford a house in this zip code. Now her children would attend the best schools, and she and David would be eligible for membership in the exclusive Kings Pointe Country Club.

Terri was glad to see that her children, Madison and Mason, easily made friends with other children in the neighborhood. Often, they invited them over to play video games or swim in the backyard pool.

One afternoon, while Terri was making a pitcher of lemonade for the gang of kids gathered around her pool, she overhead their conversation through the open kitchen window. They were obviously arguing about something, and she stopped to listen.

"Well, we just bought our Mercedes, so it's brand new, with leather seats and everything," Mason said.

"Yeah," Madison chimed in. "And it was the most expensive one at the car place."

"Well, the pool in my backyard is way bigger than this one," one of the guests retorted.

"Is not!" replied Mason and Madison in unison.

Her children's words pierced Terri's heart like arrows, and a wave of shame flooded over her. God couldn't have sent her a more powerful message that her priorities were way out of whack. She called Madison and Mason in for a long talk, knowing she also needed to schedule another long talk—one with God to put her life back in line.

It doesn't take much time around children to realize they reflect everything they hear and see—including hidden objectives. God often uses children to show us the error of our ways. Thankfully, He is also quick to forgive if we acknowledge our mistakes and set things straight.

§

Lord, I am grateful when You bless me with good things. But don't let me forget to keep even the good things in proper perspective, maintaining a humble spirit and sharing my blessings with others where I can.

A friend loves at all times.
PROVERBS 17:17

Friends are God's way of taking care of us.

THE
REUNION

IN HIGH SCHOOL, THEY WERE KNOWN AS THE "FABULOUS FOUR." Jackie, Cheryl, Marsha, and Beverly were the most popular girls at Hulen High. They were also inseparable, vowing to be best friends forever, no matter what.

That was twenty-five years ago, and when Jackie received an invitation to her upcoming class reunion, she sighed as she remembered the Fabulous Four's vow. As a matter of fact, the four girls had gone separate ways, and the phone calls and letters eventually ended. Now, Jackie had no idea where her friends were or how their lives turned out.

Two weeks before the reunion, Jackie panicked. She had visions of her former friends showing up thin and successful. Jackie was embarrassed by her plain-Jane life. She hadn't even finished college. Sure she had two wonderful children and a great marriage, but so what? She was still "just a housewife."

Jackie's fears were confirmed at the reunion. Cheryl had a Ph.D., Marsha owned her own design studio, and Beverly had been around the world—twice. But as they shared more about their lives over the past twenty-five years, Jackie also learned that Cheryl had battled cancer, Marsha had suffered bankruptcy, and Beverly had been divorced—twice.

As her friends shared the struggles they had been through, Jackie felt God touch her heart, not only with gratitude for her life as "just a house-wife" but also with a renewed love for her high school friends. And she vowed once again that she would be a best friend forever, no matter what.

Every task done well, no matter how humble, is honorable. True joy is not found in prestige or position, but rather in finding peace with all God asks, and performing to our utmost.

Lord, at times I compare myself to others and their achievements instead of being happy for them and content with my own. Forgive me for my ungrateful attitude and fill me with Your presence.

All discipline for the moment seems
not to be joyful, but sorrowful; yet to those
who have been trained by it, afterwards
it yields the peaceful fruit of righteous.
HEBREWS 12:11 NASB

When God is our strength, it is strength indeed,
but when our strength is our own it is only weakness.

STRENGTHENING THE CORE

THE NEWEST EXERCISE CRAZE, THE PILATES SYSTEM, WAS ACTUALLY DEVELOPED DURING WORLD WAR I BY JOSEPH PILATES, A GERMAN ATHLETE. While in a British internment camp, Pilates rehabilitated other internees through exercises he devised using hospital bedsprings. Remarkably, none of these patients caught the deadly influenza sweeping across Europe at the time. Doctors attributed this phenomenon to the stimulation of their immune systems through Pilates' exercises.[3]

Over the past 80 years, the Pilates System of more than 500 different exercises has become a standard in dance training studios nationwide. Now it is finding a new home among health clubs.

The system focuses on developing the muscles of the mid-section, or torso. The theory is that if the torso, the body's "power center," is strong, the movement of all other body parts is easier.

That's also true in other areas of life. If our power center, or our spiritual core, is strong, then strength will flow to the rest of our lives, and we will be immune to many of life's ills. Our finances, relationships, occupations, and emotions can be healthy if our spiritual core is well developed.

Like our physical body, we must exercise our spiritual life daily. It takes discipline to build up spiritual health. We must be dedicated to studying God's Word, developing an effective prayer life, and applying our spiritual gifts. And when we become weary, God is near to provide us with His strength to persevere and assure us that just as physical exercise pays off in a stronger, healthier body, spiritual exercise pays off in a happier, more effective life that brings honor to Him.

Just as with any physical regimen, spiritual development requires diligent effort and time spent in God's Word and in prayer. There are no shortcuts. Make spiritual exercises part of your daily routine!

§

I'm lazy, Lord, when it comes to taking care of my spiritual development. I find many excuses to keep me from focusing on You and what You want me to do with my life. Use Your Holy Spirit to coach me toward greater goals and to keep me on track.

Whoever walks with the wise will become wise.
PROVERBS 13:20 NLT

Blessed is the influence of one true, loving soul on another.

A BIG SISTER'S INFLUENCE

KELLY WASN'T SURE. Relating to teenagers intimidated her. But when she read about the Big Sisters program, she felt God urge her to apply. It sounded easy enough. She would be assigned to a girl who needed a positive, older woman's influence in her life. Then they would spend time together, going for sodas, hanging out in the mall, or other things of mutual interest.

When Kelly met 13-year-old Ashley, they were both shy, but their friendship steadily grew, and Kelly looked forward to their times together. Still she prayed, *God make me more than a friend to Ashley. Make me a good influence too.*

Although Ashley started out their relationship as a marginal student, over time her grades began to improve. Kelly was tickled when she was invited to attend an awards ceremony to see Ashley receive a pin for the highest grade in science among the 7th grade class.

As Ashley gave Kelly a tour of the school, Kelly was amused to see the open doors of girls' lockers. They were plastered with posters of teen idols, photos of friends, and notes from boyfriends. She was surprised when Ashley opened the door to her locker. Instead of teen idols, displayed inside were cards and notes of encouragement Kelly had sent to her. And right in the middle was a photo of the two of them.

Kelly was overwhelmed. As she walked arm-in-arm with Ashley to the auditorium for the awards ceremony, she felt God say, *Because of you, Ashley was motivated to do well in school. This award belongs to you too.*

Everyone has something significant to offer another. And there is always someone who can use a mentor and friend to encourage them along life's way. Plus that same someone will have something special to impart to you too.

§

Help me, Father, to not give in to my insecurities when thinking about others. It takes so little effort to be a friend, and the dividends are immeasurable. Thank You for helping me see that, and thank You for providing me with friends of all ages, sizes, colors and interests.

The righteous will live by their faith.
HABAKKUK 2:4 NLT

Great works are performed not by strength but by perseverance.

THE FAMILY BIBLE SECRET

SINCE CORINNE WAS A LITTLE GIRL LEARNING ABOUT PAUL'S MISSIONARY TRIPS AT CHURCH, SHE HAD WANTED TO SEE THE HOLY LAND. She wanted to see the ruins of Ephesus where Paul caused a riot among worshipers of Artemus; the catacombs in Rome where early Christians hid to worship; the cave on the island of Patmos where John received the Book of Revelation.

For the past five years Corinne filled a special jar labeled "Holy Land Trip Money." And whenever she had extra loose change, it went immediately into the jar. Her trip fund grew slowly. Corinne was determined.

When the pastor of her church announced he was putting together the very trip Corinne had dreamed about, she immediately signed up. But when she counted her money, she found she didn't have enough. Nevertheless, Corinne had a strong feeling that God would provide a way for her to go on the trip, and she left her name on the registration list.

Feeling melancholy, Corinne went to the attic and got the old family Bible out of a big, dusty trunk. She hadn't looked at it since she was little, but she remembered it had wonderful, colorful maps of the Holy Land.

When Corinne turned to the map section, she was startled to find tucked between the pages two one hundred-dollar bills. Her mother must have put them there for safekeeping years ago. Her heart leaped for joy—it was exactly the amount she needed for the Holy Land trip. She knew this desire in her heart was from God and she believed He was sending her—with this miracle.

The best part about God-given dreams is that with faith, determination, and diligent effort, they will come true. What's your dream? Commit it to God, work toward it, and see how He will use it to bless many.

§

Praise to the God of miracles who answers prayers in amazing and creative ways! Thank You, Lord, for giving me dreams and for making Yourself evident in ways that confirm Your presence in my life.

Throw yourselves into the work of the Master,
confident that nothing you do for him is a waste of time or effort.
1 CORINTHIANS 15:58 MSG

Growth is the only evidence of life.

GROWING UP SPIRITUALLY

IT'S A UNIVERSAL TRUTH: CHILDREN CAN'T WAIT TO GROW UP. And it's an American tradition to mark children's growth on the inside of a closet door or a special growth chart. Sometimes there's a significant space between the current mark and the previous one, indicating a big growth spurt. Sometimes the difference is not so dramatic. Nevertheless, children are eager to get to the next age, to make a higher mark on the closet door.

At some point in life, we stop wanting to get older. Perhaps it's when we see that first gray hair, or our growth begins to show less on the closet door and more on the bathroom scales. At that time, we may wish we could go backward in age, especially since our youth-oriented culture doesn't value growing older.

Fortunately, God values maturity—maturity of spirit and character. And throughout our Christian lives, His Holy Spirit abides in our hearts, ever reminding us that He measures us by a different standard, a spiritual growth chart. No matter how old we become, we should always be eager to make a higher mark on our spiritual growth chart. We should be constantly striving to reach the next milestone in our ultimate goal to become like Christ.

Growing more like Christ takes work, a constant striving to fill your life with things that promote spiritual health—like prayer, fellowship with other Christians, and the study of God's Word. But the rewards of making higher marks on your spiritual growth chart are more than worth it!

Growth is the evidence of life, and without nurturing our spiritual lives each day, we die a spiritual death. To avoid such a devastating experience, commit to making prayer, fellowship, and Bible study a vital part of your spiritual strengthening and development.

ॐ

Forgive me, Father, when I rush through my day without so much as a thought to drawing near to You in prayer. Without Your Word and the daily encouragement of believers, my spirit grows weary, depleted, and anemic. Revitalize me through Your Holy Spirit to grow spiritually healthy each day.

In one hour such great riches came to nothing.
REVELATION 18:17 NKJV

God evidently does not intend us all to be rich or powerful or great, but He does intend us all to be friends.

AN UNCONDITIONAL FRIENDSHIP

SHELLEY AND NICOLE AGREED THAT THE AREA BETWEEN THEIR HOUSES WAS UGLY. It was a vast expanse of rock with a rampant weed problem. Since the area was on both neighbors' property, they agreed to split the cost of turning it into a garden, complete with a gazebo and fountain.

Shelley and Nicole spent hours shopping at local greenhouses and interviewing landscapers. When the garden was completed, they were both thrilled with the results. The problem came when Shelley, who had paid for the project up front, presented a bill for half the expenses to her neighbor. Nicole agreed to pay Shelley for her half of the project as soon as possible.

Two years later, Nicole still had not reimbursed Shelley. Shelley's husband, Mike, was furious. He suggested they take their neighbors to small claims court, and he quit even saying "hi" to them when they crossed paths.

Shelley, on the other hand, felt God tell her to forget the debt and continue to treat Nicole as a friend. It was difficult, but Shelley consistently felt God's gentle nudge, *Don't worry about the money. Your testimony of unconditional love to Nicole is more important.*

One afternoon while Shelley trimmed the bushes, Nicole joined her in the garden. She handed Shelley an envelope containing the money she owed her. She said, "I'm sorry it's taken me so long to pay you back. Mostly, thank you for continuing to be my friend. Your love and support has proven to my family that the God you serve is real."

Shelley felt a Fatherly hug from heaven affirming her choice to love no matter what. She replied, "It's only money," as she gave Nicole a big hug.

When we focus on the important matters, especially in relationships, other details seem to fall into place naturally. Trust in God's sovereign power to bring all things together for His glory.

❦

God, You are the author of time. You know the beginning and the end of every story. Help me to trust You more with the little circumstances, letting go of things that are not so important in the bigger picture of life.

Those who know your name will trust in you;
for you, Lord, have never forsaken those who seek you.
PSALM 9:10

May your troubles in the coming
New Year be as short-lived as your resolutions.

A SURPRISING RESOLUTION

IT WAS THE ANNUAL "GIRLS ONLY" NEW YEAR'S EVE PARTY. CONNIE AND HER FRIENDS ALWAYS GOT TOGETHER TO CELEBRATE THE START OF THE NEW YEAR. They shared their triumphs and disappointments of the past year, and then they rang in the new year by praying for each other's resolutions.

This year, Connie's resolution was to become more organized. But when it came her turn to share her resolve for the next 12 months, she said instead, "My resolution is to look for a new job." Everyone looked at her in surprise. Connie loved her job as an account executive for a prominent advertising agency. She had brought in dozens of new accounts since she started, and she was definitely the agency's star. Connie herself was surprised that she felt led, at the last minute, to change her resolution. Nevertheless, when she said it, she felt God's confirmation in her heart.

The next Monday, not really sure why, Connie began to look for another job. Within the month, she landed a position at a different agency. She went in to talk to her boss, but before she could break the news, he said, "Connie, I'm glad you stopped in. I've put off telling you, but the agency hasn't been doing so well. It looks like we're headed for bankruptcy."

Connie could hardly believe it. She was sad the agency she had come to love was not going to make it. But she was grateful God had given her a divine "heads up" to find another position.

Change is inevitable. New beginnings are around every corner, if we're willing to venture there. But change goes much smoother when we are perceptive to God's leading. Stay tuned in to God.

§

Thank You, Lord, for preparing the way ahead of me. Help me to remain pliable to Your direction and always willing to let go of the old in order to grab onto the new. With You leading the way, change holds no fear for me.

This is my command: Love one
another the way I loved you.
JOHN 15:12 MSG

They will know we are Christians by our love.

WHAT'S YOUR MESSAGE?

BUMPER STICKERS COVER THE GAMUT. They can express your religious beliefs, political preferences, favorite radio stations, or even how your child performed in middle school. They can be funny, thought-provoking, flippant, or even rude and offensive. It's interesting to notice a bumper sticker then pull up alongside the car and observe the driver. Do you ever draw conclusions about the kind of person driving a car based on the bumper stickers?

A symbol often found on cars owned by Christians is the sign of the fish. Recently, it's become common to see on cars owned by Christians two large fish symbols, representing the parents, displayed along with as many smaller fish symbols as there are children in the family. And not just on our vehicles, but also in our jewelry and clothing, Christian symbols are commonplace. Along with the cross and sign of the fish, slogans like "W.W.J.D." to remind the wearer to consider "What Would Jesus Do?" are seen on everything from T-shirts to bracelets to, yes, bumper stickers.

But when Jesus talked about how the world would recognize that we are Christians, He didn't say that others would know us by our jewelry or T-shirts or bumper stickers. He said that others would know we are Christians by our love for each other. If we seek His Spirit, whose presence is always near, we will be able to show the same unconditional, self-sacrificing kind of love for others that He showed for us. It is then that our Christian commitment will be obvious to the world. We won't need bumper stickers to show our devotion to Christ—our very lives will proclaim it.

No one should ever have to wonder if you're a Christian. A Christian's identity is always based on love and needs to be evident to all. Love is the only calling card you will ever need.

§

May my love for You, God, and Your Kingdom, be apparent in all that I say, all that I do, and all that I am.

I myself have gained much joy and comfort
from your love, . . . because your kindness
has so often refreshed the hearts of God's people.
PHILEMON 7 NLT

The cold world needs warm-hearted Christians.

THE DOOR-TO-DOOR SALESMAN

THROUGH THE PEEPHOLE, NATALIE SAW A YOUNG MAN LOADED WITH DISPLAY CASES, OBVIOUSLY A SALESMAN. Normally, she would have ignored him until he went to bug someone else. But he looked tired, and Natalie felt sorry for him. She felt God prompt her to open the door.

When she invited him in, the young man didn't waste any time pulling out samples of "the world's best household cleaner." Natalie could barely get a word in edgewise, but when she did, she asked him if he would like a glass of iced tea.

At Natalie's kindness, the young man, named Robert, dropped his sales pitch and opened up. He explained he had been selling door to door for two weeks, but with little success. He was on the brink of giving up.

Natalie, who bought two bottles of cleaner, encouraged Robert to give it another week. And before he left, she prayed with him that his efforts would be rewarded.

Years later, Natalie received a letter in the mail from Robert. It contained a check for $500. In the letter, Robert explained that her kindness and prayer had encouraged him not to quit his sales job. Over time, he worked his way up to the position of sales director, and the enclosed check was part of the bonus he received for exceeding company sales goals.

"I wouldn't be here if it weren't for you," he wrote. Needless to say, Natalie was grateful she had listened to God and opened her door to a young, discouraged door-to-door salesman named Robert.

It takes so little to make a great difference in a person's day. Remember, Jesus loves everyone who crosses our path or comes to our door so much that He gave His life for each one. How can we ignore that?

§

Father, thank You for helping me realize that kindness costs me nothing, yet pays incredible dividends to those on the receiving end. Thank You for those who have been kind to me when I needed it most.

Rejoice in the Lord always . . . Rejoice!
Let your gentleness be evident to all. The Lord is near.
PHILIPPIANS 4:4-5

Love divine, all loves excelling; joy of heaven, to earth come down.

THE MUSIC BOX

MILLIE AND ELLIE WERE IDENTICAL TWINS. They not only looked alike, but their mother dressed them alike, and they did everything together. Eventually, they went to the same college and were roommates.

One of their favorite possessions was an exquisite music box their grandmother had given them when they were three years old. It had a delicate ballerina in a pink tutu that twirled to the music, Beethoven's "Für Elise," when the lid was opened. They weren't sure when the music box had quit playing and the ballerina stopped twirling, but even broken, it remained one of the twins' treasures, occupying a place of prominence on their dorm room dresser.

Then the unthinkable happened. Ellie was killed in a car accident. Millie, who had just missed being in the same car, was beyond grief. Without her twin she felt like one of her arms or legs were cut off. Every difficult day that followed, she prayed God would provide His comfort and healing to her broken heart.

Millie reached for something she thought might comfort her—the music box. When she opened the lid, she was amazed to hear the old, familiar tune play and see the ballerina twirl as she did years before.

Millie cried for joy as peace flooded her heart. She knew God brought the music box back to life to tell her He was watching over her. She felt His deep comfort and her grief began to abate from that day on.

In the blink of an eye, our entire life can change. Everything we've ever known can be different. But one thing is sure: Our God who is never changing will dry our eyes and pick us up. He will hear from heaven and wipe away every tear.

§

Without You, Lord, I couldn't find the courage to go on when the trials of this world lay me low. You're the one constant in my life. You give me a safe place to be, no matter the circumstances. You bring joy when I need it most. Thank You.

The word of God is living and active.
Sharper than any double-edged sword . . .
it judges the thoughts and attitudes of the heart.
HEBREWS 4:12

To be ignorant of the Scripture is not to know Christ.

HEAVEN'S WARNING SYSTEMS

HAVE YOU EVER STOPPED TO CONSIDER HOW MANY WARNING SYSTEMS THERE ARE IN LIFE? The buzzer in your car reminds you to buckle up. A different one reminds you to take your keys out of the ignition. A yellow traffic light alerts you to prepare to stop. An alarm in your home tells you that there's a fire. Flashing red lights warn you to pull over to let an ambulance go by.

Of course, you can ignore life's warning signs. You can keep going when the needle on the gas gauge hits "E." But before long, you'll be stuck on the side of the road. You can park in a "no parking" zone, but you'll have to pay a fine to get your car out of the impound lot. You can try to go around the security system at the airport, but . . . you get the idea.

For other areas of life, God provides us with two important warning systems. The first is His Word. Scripture warns us about the dangers of materialism, of dishonest business practices, of sinful relationships, and even of gossip.

The second is His Holy Spirit, our heart's constant companion and guide. Not only is the Holy Spirit your source of comfort and courage, but He is also your warning system, prodding your conscience when you are in danger of straying from the path of righteousness. God wants you to pay attention to these heavenly warning systems, just as you do flashing red lights and alarms—they're for your protection and good!

Armed with the Word of God and equipped with the fellowship of the Holy Spirit, we are prepared for anything life presents. Let us not fail to embrace the Bible's important lessons, and be thankful for God's protection throughout the journey.

God, You have given me the great gifts of Your Word and Your Spirit to sustain me and keep me from going astray. Thank You for being my consistent source of hope and love through the trials of life.

Rejoice always; pray without ceasing;
in everything give thanks; for this is
God's will for you in Christ Jesus.
1 THESSALONIANS 5:16-18 NASB

When we learn to offer up every duty connected with our life as a
sacrifice to God, a settled employment becomes just a settled habit
of prayer.

A LESSON IN PRAYER

DAYS AS A HOSPITAL PATIENT DEFINITELY CRAMPED
IRENE'S STYLE. A widow for several years, her children all grown and
gone, Irene spent her time volunteering for worthwhile causes. She
worked three days a week at the local hospice, two days at a day care center, and weekends at her church.

Since Irene's recovery was expected to take at least a month, she
needed something useful to occupy her while in the hospital. She made
a list of everyone she knew—from family members to church friends to
the hospital staff—and began to pray for them. She had her schedule
precisely planned so each person on her list received quality prayer time.

Before long, Irene began to hear stories of how God worked in the
lives of those for whom she prayed. Her niece received a full college
scholarship. Her friend Hazel's arthritis was much better. Her son-in-law
finally accepted Christ as his personal Savior. Her nurse received a long-

anticipated pay increase.

When Irene's doctor finally told her she could go home in the next day or so, she thought, *Too bad I won't have time to pray like I've had here in the hospital.* Before the thought was barely even formed, God responded to her heart, *You'll have the same 24 hours each day you've had in the hospital. Continue to make time to pray!*

When she left the hospital, Irene looked forward to getting back to her regular schedule, with the addition of one more task—to pray without ceasing.

Why is it we never seem to have time for prayer until we have nothing but time? Make prayer a daily priority for a lifetime.

§

Though I may often forget to begin my day in conversation with You, Lord, You never fail to include me in Yours. Forgive my lack of attention to You. I need You every day, and I don't want to begin another one without first talking it over with You.

He remembered that they were merely mortal,
gone in a moment like a breath of wind, never to return.
PSALM 78:39 NLT

In the presence of eternity, the mountains are as transient as the clouds.

SNAPSHOT ENCOUNTERS

HAVE YOU EVER NOTICED THE "OTHER PEOPLE" IN YOUR PHOTOGRAPHS? They are those who inadvertently end up in your vacation snapshots and family albums for all posterity. On the other hand, have you ever wondered how many photos of complete strangers you are in? Of course, we always try to avoid being in the way when someone takes that once-in-a-lifetime shot of the kids at the Grand Canyon or the Empire State Building. But often, we wander into those shots completely unaware. It's just for a second when we're in the line of the camera's sights, but it often happens to be the very second that the shutter clicks.

Make a point to notice how many people wander into your life, even for just a second—the checkout person at the grocery store, the paper carrier collecting for the month, the teller at the bank. You can create special moments for these people who happen across your path. A sunny smile, a comment about a job well done, an effort to hold the door open for someone whose arms are full. These are small, snapshot encounters, yet they can turn an entire day around for someone feeling unappreciated and unnoticed.

As much as we try to plan and control our lives, the truth is there are hundreds of unplanned, candid moments each and every day. When you pay attention, God's ever-present Holy Spirit can make you aware of these moments. And He encourages you to make the most of each one because you never know when you may end up in someone's album of permanent memories.

We realize our lives are but a second in the larger scheme of time, but the moments we share with one another will last forever in our hearts and souls. Make each moment count for something—you never know what it may mean to another's day.

§

We are finite, Lord; You are infinite. You are the alpha and the omega of all time, space and history. And though my portion of time is brief, I pray it will bring joy and love to as many people as possible, and to Your glory.

*We're not giving up. How could we! Even though
on the outside it often looks like things are falling apart on us,
on the inside, where God is making new life,
not a day goes by without his unfolding grace.*
2 CORINTHIANS 4:16 MSG

God always answers our prayer. Either He changes the circumstances, or He supplies sufficient power to overcome them.

HAPPY
EVER AFTER

SAMANTHA COPED WITH LIFE BY PAINTING. When she became engaged five years ago, she had no idea her husband-to-be would turn into an alcoholic. Like so many women in Samantha's situation, she was afraid to leave. She had no means of income, no self-esteem, and now she was pregnant.

So with a cheap set of paints and brushes bought at the local discount store, Samantha began to paint pictures of the ideal life. Her paintings had houses with white picket fences, bright suns, and happy children playing. While she painted, Samantha also prayed. As a new Christian, she asked God for help.

One day while painting, Samantha felt God tell her that she was in danger and should leave immediately. She quickly packed a few clothes and her paintings, and left before her husband returned in an alcoholic rage.

While staying with a family from her church, Samantha racked her brain. How in the world was she going to support herself and the baby? *Your paintings,* God told her heart. *Sell your paintings.*

Samantha didn't think her paintings were worth anything, but she had nothing to lose and took a few to a gallery. The owner loved Samantha's simple, but honest and winsome style. He was delighted to display her paintings, which sold quickly.

Samantha soon made more than enough money to support herself and her baby girl. She continued to paint houses and suns and happy children, but she found that painting with God produced the most wonderful canvasses of art—much like her own life had become with each precious brushstroke by His hand.

Despite the bad circumstances we may face, God redeems anyone who seeks His face and His direction for a new chance. Jesus died on a cross so all who call on Him could be released from sin. Look to Him for the hope and the promise of a new life.

§

Lord, I've made mistakes; some worse than others, but none You can't redeem. Thank You for the promise of new life through the forgiveness of sin. Thank You for protecting me from myself and giving me the hope to go on.

*"If you have faith as small as a mustard seed,
you can say to this mulberry tree, 'Be uprooted
and planted in the sea,' and it will obey you."*
LUKE 17:6

Believe that you have it, and you have it.

FAITH 101

SYDNEY WAS A GREAT KID. She was president of her youth group, one of the school's newspaper staff, and an active Spanish club member. Sydney's favorite hobby was witnessing to others. Her style of sharing was powerful, and she had a knack for presenting Christ that drew others in.

Dana was proud of her daughter, but she was also concerned when Sydney announced that she planned to attend a Bible college known for its missions program. The problem was that Sydney didn't have the grades or test scores required for admission. Dana tried to steer her daughter toward a community college that was more forgiving of her academic standing, but Sydney was determined. "I know God wants me to go to school here," she said as she completed her Bible college application. She even traveled the 500 miles to meet with the school's admissions officer personally.

Dana watched the mail, dreading the day her daughter's rejection letter arrived. When it did, she watched Sydney's face closely as she ripped open the envelope and read it to herself. Not far into the letter, Sydney let out a yell and hugged her mom. "I knew it! I knew it!"

The letter said that although Sydney didn't have the requisite grades, her meeting with the admissions officer convinced him she had all the qualities to become a great missionary. Therefore, the school would make an exception for her. Dana was impressed by the power of her daughter's faith, and through her daughter's experience she realized her own faith could use a little polishing!

Isn't it refreshing to encounter someone whose faith is naturally evident? Why isn't every believer living in such a way that their faith is something they aren't afraid to reveal? It doesn't have to be this way. When we commit to showing our faith, it's amazing to see what God will do!

§

Though You've never let me down, Lord, I hesitate to let others see my faith in You. Help me to trust You even more so my faith is evident to all.

*People who live this way make it plain
that they are looking for their true home.
If they were homesick for the old country,
they could have gone back any time they wanted.
But they were after a far better country than that
—heaven country.*

HEBREWS 11:14-16 MSG

You receive a key to heaven's gates when you receive Christ.

HEAVENLY CITIZENSHIP

EVERY YEAR, MORE THAN HALF A MILLION FOREIGN-BORN PEOPLE BECOME CITIZENS OF THE UNITED STATES THROUGH THE PROCESS KNOWN AS NATURALIZATION. These people have chosen to renounce allegiance to their former countries and become full-fledged Americans.

Naturalization is not an easy process. In addition to being at least eighteen years old and having resided in the United States for at least five years, applicants must also be able to read, write, and speak English; have knowledge of the U.S. government and history; and demonstrate good moral character. On top of that, the application process is long and involved.

Yet hundreds of thousands of people are willing to do what it takes to enjoy the freedoms of American citizenship, and there is a continual backlog of applications.

Citizenship in God's kingdom, likewise, has specific requirements. But they are simple and can be fulfilled in one sincere prayer. There is no backlog of applications for heavenly citizenship, and God accepts anyone who wants to enter.

When we chose to become citizens of God's Kingdom through salvation in Jesus Christ, like those who have become citizens of the United States, we renounced our former allegiance—in this case, our allegiance to the world. In fact, with God in our lives, we are no longer citizens of the world or subject to its temptations and pitfalls. Sometimes we forget where our spiritual citizenship lies and return to the ways of the world. At those times, God, whose presence we can always count on, reminds our hearts of our eternal citizenship and shows us the way back home, to the place where true freedom is found.

What a reassuring feeling to know, as believers, that this weary world is not our home, and that we have a permanent residence waiting for our arrival. Thanks to Jesus Christ we are not homeless aliens anymore.

§

I look forward to the day, Father, when I will make my home with You in paradise. But until then, I have work to do here so others will see You living in me. Help me to not become too attached to anything this world offers.

ENDNOTES

1 Richard Stevenson, "A Buried Message Loudly Heard," New York Times, 7 December 1996, pages 19, 21.

2 www.walmartstores.com

3 www.pilatesberlin.de/en/jp.htm

ACKNOWLEDGEMENTS

Anonymous (6, 14, 16, 18, 38, 46, 78, 104, 106, 108, 110, 118, 120. 126, 130, 138, 144, 160, 164, 174, 186, 188, 190, 200, 204), Russian Proverb (10), Soren Kierkgaard (12), Harriet Beecher Stowe (20), Spanish Proverb (22, 146), Blaise Pascal (24, 68), Victor Hugo (26), Henry Ward Beecher (28), Francis de Sales (30), Frederick W. Faber (32), Greek Proverb (34), Jewish Proverb (36, 44, 96), St. Augustine Hippo (40, 176), Johann Wolfgang von Goethe (42), Terese of Lisieux (48), Henry David Thoreau (50, 162), Horatius Bonar (52), English Proverb (54, 90, 198), William Cowper (56, 158), Teresa of Avila (58), John Watson (60), Thomas Jefferson (62), John Keats (64), G. K. Chesteron (66), Robert A. Cook (70), Wendell Phillips (72), Jacques Ellul (74), John Churton Collins (76), Theophane Venard (80), T. S. Mathews (82), Ambrose (84), Thales (86), Albert Einstein (88), John Quincy Adams (92), William Law (94), Horace Bushnell (98), John Ferguson (100), Maria Thusick (102), Woodrow Wilson (112), Franklin P. Jones (114), Turkish Proverb (116), Ralph Waldo Emerson (122, 124, 184), Dwight L. Moody (128, 168), Latin proverb (132), William Blake (134), Vincent Van Gogh (136), George MacDonald (140), Thomas Pope Blount (142), Cherokee Saying (148), William Shakespeare (150), Richard of Chichester (152), Aristotle (156), John of Damascus (166), John Wesley (170), Andrew Carnegie (172), George Elliot (178), Samuel Johnson (180), John Henry Newman (182), Charles Wesley (192), Jerome (194), Thomas Erskine (196), John Keats (198), Desiderius Erasmus (202).

Additional copies of this title and other titles from Honor Books are available from your local bookstore.

God's Hand on My Shoulder
God's Hand on My Shoulder for Teens

If you have enjoyed this book,
or if it has impacted your life,
we would like to hear from you.

Please contact us at:

Honor Books,
An Imprint of Cook Communications Ministries
4050 Lee Vance View
Colorado Springs, CO 80918

Or through our website:

www.cookministries.com